PETER
FINDS
PURPOSE

DARYL T SANDERS

This book is a result of a personal Bible study where I reviewed 1ST AND 2ND Peter and looked at these epistles in light of them being the last will and testament of the pioneer leader of the church.

When a pioneer comes to the end of the trail and looks back he will give us words and principles to live by and Peter does just that. Peter is able to articulate the purpose of it all – **it is not what you do for God it is who you are for God that counts.**

You may contact me at 12dsanders@gmail.com for speaking engagements or questions or discussion.

Other books by Daryl T Sanders are:

Peter Finds Life (Peter in the Gospels)
Peter Finds Power (Peter in the Book of Acts)
God the Father (Why does He use this Name?)
WHY – Questions along life's journey
Finding the Power to Heal
David, Chosen by God

All Bible references used the New King James Version as found on the web site www.blueletterbible.org. Definitions are from Strong's Concordance.

Table of Contents

CHAPTER ONE
1 PETER 1

We must remember that Peter was a member of the inner circle of Jesus. He was there for every miracle performed by Jesus. He was a participant in walking on water, and raising the dead with Jesus taking the lead. He was the one who spoke up at every confusing turn, sometimes questioning the wisdom of Jesus and was disciplined for it. Jesus was quick to respond whenever wrong thinking was evidenced by Peter.

Peter was also the first one to "catch on." He was the one who first realized Jesus was the Messiah. He was also the one who recognized that there was an enablement from heaven that empowered man to do things contrary to the accepted laws of nature. He found that this "anointing" from heaven could be "tapped into" by faith.

This "tapping in" process has been lost for the most part in the church. Somewhere along the way the church started rationalizing why or when they could not get the sick healed and the dead raised. Out of this rationalization mentality rose up the spectator mentality that seems to prevail in the western church.

What we must see, because it is at work in virtually all third world evangelistic efforts, is that the miraculous did not disappear from the arsenal of the church efforts to win the lost. Rather we have built a strange theology around the times "it did not work that accommodates failure." Church leaders became so concerned when they prayed for the sick and the sick did not get well that they had to give an account for "it not working!"

Well, in those instances we can say for some reason I could not get them well, so it was either my fault or maybe I did something wrong. Another and easier explanation – after all why would I take the blame if I don't have to – maybe it wasn't God's will to get this person that I prayed for healed!

Yes, that's the mysterious "God's will" conundrum. Who can question that, after all who can say without a doubt that this or that is or is not God's will?

So here we are 2,000 years later and the theologians have constructed a theology that is summed up like this prayer: "God, if it is in your will please somehow heal this person. Of course if it is not your will, that's ok too, and we accept that."

The problem with this theology is that there is no scriptural basis for it. As in none no not one! Jesus prayed for the sick directly nineteen times in His ministry here on earth. Every single one He prayed for was healed. There is not one person who was not healed during the earthly ministry of Jesus. I would imagine that one example would have been given to show that healing is not always possible.

He prayed as the Man Christ Jesus not as the God Christ Jesus. In other words, He prayed under the same circumstances and the same authority that each believer has today.

To make this point more dramatic, we do not find one instance where Peter prayed for the sick and they did not get healed. So we lose the argument that somehow Jesus had the anointing or enablement but maybe we don't.

There is a little understood principle that also applies to the working of the anointing or enablements of God. It may at first sound heretical but see for yourself. We can have influence with God by our own very presence and concern for the situation to the point that God will do it because we ask Him to do it.

Ezek 14:13-14 *"Son of man, when a land sins against Me by persistent unfaithfulness, I will stretch out My hand against it; I will cut off its supply of bread, send famine on it, and cut off man and beast from it. Even IF these three men, Noah, Daniel, and Job, were in it, they would deliver ONLY themselves by their righteousness,"* says the Lord GOD.

Here we see that God even names three people, from three different eras that He recognized for their faith that could influence what happened on earth. Our current theology does not seem to take into account that God has called us and enabled us to find life – eternal life – in Christ Jesus. And then at the same time He has enabled us power – Holy Spirit Power, which enables us to exercise authority over this earthly kingdom and what happens here.

This is a lost concept so let me bear down on it. In the above passage in Ezekiel God is saying in essence, that these three men generally had the God given authority to make happen on earth what "they" – not necessarily God - but what they wanted done. The passage is saying that however is not always true because the people may have gone too far and are due judgment that no amount of intercession is going to stop that judgment.

Before we get too riled up with these statements let me acknowledge the mystery that still surrounds both healing power and intervention over the earthly realm. When Jesus healed the man at the Pool of Bethesda He stepped over many sick to get to the one God was going to heal. We do not know all the conditions and cause and effects that are in place. We do know however, that believers who can tap into the anointing and can exercise this power can walk in faith without fear and doubting.

Before we move forward let us take a look at this scripture that will give further insight into the issue of sickness and healing:

Phil 2:25-27 *Yet I considered it necessary to send to you Epaphroditus, my brother, fellow worker, and fellow soldier, but your messenger and the one who ministered to my need; since he was longing for you all, and was distressed because you had heard that he was sick. For indeed he was sick almost unto death; but God had mercy on him, and not only on him but on me also, lest I should have sorrow upon sorrow.*

The significance here is that there are sicknesses that may befall us. And that we do not have a magic wand that "works every time." There is still a mercy and grace from God that comes into play. There is still some measure of mystery surrounding sickness and disease and the causes and effects at work.

BUT, we must take a more proactive role in faith looking and expecting that the power of God is available and then exercising ourselves in faith to pray the healing prayers for the saints. Each believer needs to learn how to "tap into" this place of faith and use it.

Now let's move forward. Peter not only was a part of the inner circle. Peter was the early first leader of the church. When we just take a look at the highlights they are quite remarkable.

In the Book of Acts:

- He preached the first sermon – and saved 3,000
- Healed the first sick person – and saved 5,000
- He exercised apostolic authority
- His shadow healed all the sick that came under it
- He prayed for the sick in regions and they all were healed
- He argued in court for the cause of Christ
- He laid hands on new believers for the Baptism in the Holy Spirit

- He was the first to preach to the Gentiles
- He followed an angel out of prison
- He argued before the apostles to accept Gentile believers
- He raised the dead

After having done all of these exploits he was now coming to the end of his life. He is getting ready to tell us his last words. We will see that he does not tell us what to do for God. He does not tell us how to organize the church. He does not give us directions for evangelizing the world.

1 Peter 1: (text of the chapter)

Peter, an apostle of Jesus Christ, To the pilgrims of the Dispersion in Pontus, Galatia, Cappadocia, Asia, and Bithynia, elect according to the foreknowledge of God the Father, in sanctification of the Spirit, for obedience and sprinkling of the blood of Jesus Christ: Grace to you and peace be multiplied.

A Heavenly Inheritance

Blessed BE the God and Father of our Lord Jesus Christ, who according to His abundant mercy has begotten us again to a living hope through the resurrection of Jesus Christ from the dead, to an inheritance incorruptible and undefiled and that does not fade away, reserved in heaven for you, who are kept by the power of God through faith for salvation ready to be revealed in the last time.

In this you greatly rejoice, though now for a little while, if need be, you have been grieved by various trials, that the genuineness of your faith, BEING much more precious than gold that perishes, though it is tested by fire, may be found to praise, honor, and glory at the revelation of Jesus Christ, whom having not seen you love. Though now you do not see HIM, yet believing, you rejoice with joy inexpressible and full of glory, receiving the end of your faith—the salvation of YOUR souls.

Of this salvation the prophets have inquired and searched carefully, who prophesied of the grace THAT WOULD COME to you, searching what, or what manner of time, the Spirit of Christ who was in them was indicating when He testified beforehand the sufferings of Christ and the glories that would follow. To them it was revealed that, not to themselves, but to us they were ministering the things which now have been reported to you through those who have preached the gospel to you by the Holy Spirit sent from heaven—things which angels desire to look into.

Living Before God Our Father

Therefore gird up the loins of your mind, be sober, and rest YOUR hope fully upon the grace that is to be brought to you at the revelation of Jesus Christ; as obedient children, not conforming yourselves to the former lusts, AS in your ignorance; but as He who called you IS holy, you also be holy in all YOUR conduct, because it is written, "BE HOLY, FOR I AM HOLY."

And if you call on the Father, who without partiality judges according to each one's work, conduct yourselves throughout the time of your stay HERE in fear; knowing that you were not redeemed with corruptible things, LIKE silver or gold, from your aimless conduct RECEIVED by tradition from your fathers, but with the precious blood of Christ, as of a lamb without blemish and without spot. He indeed was foreordained before the foundation of the world, but was manifest in these last times for you who through Him believe in God, who raised Him from the dead and gave Him glory, so that your faith and hope are in God.

The Enduring Word

Since you have purified your souls in obeying the truth through the Spirit in sincere love of the brethren, love one another fervently with a pure heart, having been born again, not of corruptible seed but incorruptible, through the word of God which lives and abides forever, because "ALL FLESH IS AS GRASS, AND ALL THE GLORY OF MAN AS THE FLOWER OF THE GRASS. THE GRASS WITHERS, AND ITS FLOWER FALLS AWAY, BUT THE WORD OF THE LORD ENDURES FOREVER."

Now this is the word which by the gospel was preached to you.

It is good to read Peter's epistles in light of the fact that he knows that his own end is near. Jesus told him that he would suffer a martyr's death for his faith.

If we can sum up Peter's main emphasis it would be first and foremost in both of his epistles that our fulfillment in life is *not in what we do for God but who we are in Christ*.

Peter, thirty plus years after his early experiences in the Book of Acts, starts writing his "last words and testament." It seems very important that we consider his words in the context that after it was all said and done, here is his legacy to the church. By this time in the life of the church, he had seen it all and he had lived it all. He saw what worked and what failed and certainly lived his own ups and downs. He had seen good teachers and bad teachers. He had seen good times and times of persecution. He had seen many plans and ideas come forth.

When a Patriarch of a family is on his deathbed so to speak, let every member of the family take note. What he says in his last days is said for no other reason than what is in each member of the family's own best interest. He has no personal agenda. He is not trying to get us to go along with something he just wants to do. He is passing on those plans and principles that are for our good.

On one hand we can even say that he is telling us that if he had it to do all over again these would be the things he would concentrate on all the time and let all the other stuff fall by the way side.

He addresses the readers as strangers – and this is an important perspective. We are no longer earthbound after we become a believer. Our address is in heaven now and we are here on earth just as the first pilgrims were on the shores of the United States. We have an agenda that is laid out for us and that is we are to be witnesses of His mercy and grace and truth in this troubled world.

Then Peter testifies that as his life comes to a close he looks forward to his inheritance. There is a heaven and it is reserved for believers. He acknowledges that we can't keep ourselves in the faith, but testifies we are kept by the power of God. He tells us that the way God keeps us is by our faith holding on to the promises of God's salvation to all that believe. In other words, it is not us just passively going through life assuming that one day we go to heaven. But rather it is us living our lives as best we can believing that He is keeping us and holding on to us to the end.

Peter goes on to promote a regular part of our life is to be done in praising and rejoicing in God. While in the same breath he acknowledges the testing that will be a part of our life in faith. The word "rejoicing" actually means by definition- "jumping for joy," or even "spinning around." Somewhere along the history of the church we turned rejoicing into words only. Solemnity in the church was never the regular part of the early church, and Peter was a leading proponent of regular, physical expression of worship in the church. If we take the words literally here – he says "greatly" rejoice. That means go for it, go all out, jump for joy like you mean it and you want everyone else to see that you mean it.

Let's consider the warning of the testing he is talking about. This is not merely persecution by others (although it includes that). But our faith is tested in daily living when we are given ample opportunity to operate in the flesh. But if we will hold on to our faith and refuse the temptations the world continually offers to us and realize that the rewards from heaven are greater than any momentary fun in the flesh.

Of course, remember that Peter himself was told by Jesus that Jesus prayed that Peter's faith would not fail in Peter's time of testing. So here we have Peter turning around and teaching us that our faith will be tested – accept the fact – face the fact – and be ready to hold on for dear life and live the fact that although you will be tested He will hold onto you and carry you through every fiery trial you may endure.

At the same time there will be persecution for our faith. The altar of heaven is the covering for those who have been martyred for their faith. It has been said more Christians have died for the cause of their faith in Christ in the last twenty years than in the last 2000 years. Over two million Christians have died in Sudan alone in the last twenty years – just because they are Christians and would not renounce their faith.

Stephen was the first martyr of the church. When we take note of the event it says that as he was being stoned, he looked up and the veil of heaven was folded back. Acts 7 says that as he looked up he saw Jesus "standing" on the right hand of the throne. The Bible tells us in other places that Jesus is "seated" at the right hand of the Father. This means Jesus stood up to welcome, the first martyr and to assure all the future martyrs that their death is not in vain.

Peter goes on to remind us of the suffering of Jesus on our behalf. In essence, after he tells us that we will suffer at times it will be just as Jesus suffered at times. Again Peter clarifies good theology that is important to the Jews. As we have seen – does the Messiah come in glory or suffer first? Here Peter declares that most have missed the prophetic declaration that the Messiah had to first come to suffer for our sins before He could come again in all His glory.

Peter than tells clearly the thrust of his message and challenges every believer. Regardless of suffering, regardless of what life brings your way, you must live this life in holiness. The Patriarch is telling the church of the ages that we can rejoice in our faith, our faith will be tested, some will suffer – but so did Jesus, but that above it all we must live our lives in holiness.

As we see throughout First and Second Peter the theme is the same. To repeat this theme - *Life is not about what we do for Christ but who we are in Christ.* Life is not about what we accomplish but about what we become. He reminds us that judgment is coming. Our present generation seems to have lost the sense of accountability. Our culture in America actually teaches that there are not any consequences for our actions. In fact, when we do the wrong things the prevailing psychology is let's look back in our life to see who we can blame for us deciding to do the wrong things. It must be someone else's fault!

The debate over education regarding evolution or creation is not about science. It is about accountability. Since there is a Creator - then those that He creates must face the fact that the creature is accountable to the Creator. The public school system and many scientists won't go there so they hold onto the evolution side of the debate. There is not one proven truth in evolution! Note this quote from http://www.acgr.org/

Colin Patterson, Senior Paleontologist at London Museum of Natural History

"The question is: *Can you tell me anything you know about evolution, any one thing....that is true?* I tried that question on the geology staff at the Field Museum of Natural History and the only answer I got was silence. I tried it on the members of the Evolutionary Morphology Seminar at the University of Chicago, a very prestigious body of evolutionists, and all I got there was silence for a long time, and eventually one person said, 'I do know one thing-- it ought not to be taught in high school.' "

Regardless of man's creative methods to avoid the
concept of judgment – judgment is truly coming. Peter
ties holiness – judgment – and fear together in a few
verses. Peter is telling us to live our lives in holiness.
He is saying God is holy and wants and expects us to be
holy. There is a day of judgment coming for all. So
pass your days here in fear – meaning let fear keep you
on your toes that you would live right for God regardless
of testing and persecutions and for that matter
opportunity for the flesh.

When we stop and consider the context of last words
written by a Patriarch, one would expect to be told how
to succeed. In our western culture especially we are
focused on accomplishment. Achievement in the
Kingdom of God on earth is not a valid measurement of
one's personal success. Because everything we do
"achieve" has been done via the power of the Holy Spirit
working in and through us. Advancing the Kingdom of
God on earth is not about us it is about Him. As has
been preached many a time God will speak through a
donkey if need be to get His message through to people!

So we see then that Peter declares that Christianity is not
about building churches or saving thousands or any other
grandiose things, but rather that we should live Holy as
He is Holy.

The essence of our faith message- we have been
redeemed by the Blood of the Lamb, who lived perfect
on earth, and it is now by Him that we believe in God.
Notice how it ties together- The Plan of Salvation was

established before the foundations of the world were put in place. It was known that man would fail, so the Plan included the Messiah to come, live as a man – but – in perfection, He would die, and his sacrificial blood were payment for the sins of man, He would rise from the dead – and this resurrection is our proof that his sacrifice was acceptable, and now when we believe in God who sent Him we find our hope for eternity.

This life is short – the older one gets the more this truth is understood. When you are ten years old, one year is a long time – it is after all ten percent of your life. But when you are fifty years old one year is only two percent of your life. Since one day is as a thousand years to God, this would represent that a seventy year old person is the equivalent of having lived fifty nine minutes!

The years, regardless of perspective are short and life is fleeting but eternity goes forever and ever. The comfort we have is the word of the Lord endures forever. When we can grasp the truth of how limited our time really is on this planet we can begin to understand we should only have time for the important (to God) and eternal to us really matters.

I have often said to groups, "Think back to five years ago, and what was it that kept you up at night or that you were focused on as a major problem in your life. Is that same thing going on in your life today?" The answer from thousands of people asked is virtually one hundred percent- no. Meaning that most of the things we worry about or get preoccupied with in life don't even matter for a few years let alone eternity. Usually the problems of life go away and new problems come into play as we try to get along and move forward in a dysfunctional (read sinful) world.

Let's consider the hospital bed example. When someone gets real sick and not sure of the prognosis whether life or death is coming - priorities suddenly and with force get realigned. Jobs, money, house, sex, pleasure, vacation, TV, dinner, golf, or sports of any kind, what someone said to you or about you, just doesn't matter at a time like that. The sense to finish up and tie loose ends with family and friends rises in importance. A repentive attitude fills one's heart at moments like this. Making sure we are "right with God" moves to the top of the list.

Peter is in essence telling us act like every day you are on your death bed! After we accept Christ as our Savior we then gain a heavenly address. Consider what Paul said about this concept to the Philippians:

Phil 3:16-21 *Nevertheless, to THE DEGREE that we have already attained, let us walk by the same rule, let us be of the same mind.*

Brethren, join in following my example, and note those who so walk, as you have us for a pattern. For many walk, of whom I have told you often, and now tell you even weeping, THAT THEY ARE the enemies of the cross of Christ: whose end IS destruction, whose god IS THEIR belly, and WHOSE glory IS in their shame—who set their mind on earthly things.

For our citizenship is in heaven, from which we also eagerly wait for the Savior, the Lord Jesus Christ, who will transform our lowly body that it may be conformed to His glorious body, according to the working by which He is able even to subdue all things to Himself.

Paul is saying that while we are here on earth at the same time we are citizens of heaven. In other words we are here on a passport. We do not belong to this earth. Therefore our behavior or manner of living should be measured by heavenly standards. We can get caught up to what is happening to us locally, but we should keep true to the standards required by our home allegiance – which is heaven.

We keep struggling with perspective. We accept too much by what we see and feel as determining what is important and what is not. The true perspective is that we are on a journey that will lead us to many people, places, and things. But we will go home, and all of our decisions and actions should keep in mind our responsibilities to home in all we say, and do, and go to.

Eph 2:4-6 *But God, who is rich in mercy, because of His great love with which He loved us, even when we were dead in trespasses, made us alive together with Christ (by grace you have been saved), and raised US up together, and made US sit together in the heavenly PLACES in Christ Jesus,*

Consider further Paul's letter to the Ephesians above. He is saying that we already have a heavenly address!

As previously noted Isaiah said seven hundred years before Christ that the people of his time were healed by the fact that Jesus would suffer stripes or lashes on His back. In other words what he prophesied was going to happen already happened in that it's happening to come was as sure as if it already happened.

Likewise while we are going to heaven physically sometime soon, in the reality of the Kingdom of God, we are already there! Since we are already of heaven the early church leadership of Peter and Paul drives the point home – they challenged us to act like it.

We must all look at our own lives and determine who or what is determining what we say, think, and do. In other words who or what is governing our actions? Our problem is that we virtually never stop to think about such things. We suffer a passive/aggressive lifestyle in which we get caught up in the current flow of life around us, without giving due consideration to our heavenly responsibilities and obligations.

CHAPTER TWO
1 PETER 2

1 Peter 2: Human Weakness - live right before God

Therefore, laying aside all malice, all deceit, hypocrisy, envy, and all evil speaking, as newborn babes, desire the pure milk of the word, that you may grow thereby, if indeed you have tasted that the Lord IS gracious.

The Chosen Stone and His Chosen People

Coming to Him AS TO a living stone, rejected indeed by men, but chosen by God AND precious, you also, as living stones, are being built up a spiritual house, a holy priesthood, to offer up spiritual sacrifices acceptable to God through Jesus Christ. Therefore it is also contained in the Scripture,

"BEHOLD, I LAY IN ZION A CHIEF CORNERSTONE, ELECT, PRECIOUS, AND HE WHO BELIEVES ON HIM WILL BY NO MEANS BE PUT TO SHAME."

Therefore, to you who believe, HE IS precious; but to those who are disobedient,

"THE STONE WHICH THE BUILDERS REJECTED HAS BECOME THE CHIEF CORNERSTONE,"

And "A STONE OF STUMBLING AND A ROCK OF OFFENSE." They stumble, being disobedient to the word, to which they also were appointed.

But you ARE a chosen generation, a royal priesthood, a holy nation, His own special people, that you may proclaim the praises of Him who called you out of darkness into His marvelous light; who once WERE not a people but ARE now the people of God, who had not obtained mercy but now have obtained mercy.

Living Before the World

Beloved, I beg YOU as sojourners and pilgrims, abstain from fleshly lusts which war against the soul, having your conduct honorable among the Gentiles, that when they speak against you as evildoers, they may, by YOUR good works which they observe, glorify God in the day of visitation.

Submission to Government

Therefore submit yourselves to every ordinance of man for the Lord's sake, whether to the king as supreme, or to governors, as to those who are sent by him for the punishment of evildoers and FOR THE praise of those who do good. For this is the will of God, that by doing good you may put to silence the ignorance of foolish men— as free, yet not using liberty as a cloak for vice, but as bondservants of God. Honor all PEOPLE. Love the brotherhood. Fear God. Honor the king.

Submission to Masters

Servants, BE submissive to YOUR masters with all fear, not only to the good and gentle, but also to the harsh. For this IS commendable, if because of conscience toward God one endures grief, suffering wrongfully. For what credit IS IT if, when you are beaten for your faults, you take it patiently? But when you do good and suffer, if you take it patiently, this IS commendable before God. For to this you were called, because Christ also suffered for us, leaving us an example, that you should follow His steps:

"WHO COMMITTED NO SIN, NOR WAS DECEIT FOUND IN HIS MOUTH";

who, when He was reviled, did not revile in return; when He suffered, He did not threaten, but committed HIMSELF to Him who judges righteously; who Himself bore our sins in His own body on the tree, that we, having died to sins, might live for righteousness—by whose stripes you were healed. For you were like sheep going astray, but have now returned to the Shepherd and Overseer of your souls.

Peter starts off this chapter by encouraging us to "lay aside" all those things we practice that bring conflict with others or are hurtful to others. He is passing off those things that we so often think we have a right to hold onto. The anger and hatefulness that we harbor against others should just be let go! Let all the psychobabble of the western church take note.

(Remember how Peter was taught to forgive his brother more than seventy times seven in a day.) We spend so much time coddling wrong attitudes and wrong behavior and Peter in essence says, "Just let it go."

A few years ago my wife and I went to Hawaii and to the Island of Kauai. We took the helicopter ride and flew over the island. We saw where they filmed the movie Jurassic Park. We saw a beautiful rainbow that was 360 degrees or a perfect circle and flew around the circle. When we got back and went into the small terminal there was a souvenir shop and they had hats and I couldn't resist buying one. On the front of the hat it said Kauai and on the back it said "Get over it."

I came home and preached a message called "Get over it." You would think I was a heretic! The essence of the message was quit hanging onto past hurts, quit holding grudges, quit revisiting damaging relationships, and get on with the life we have in Christ Jesus. That stirred up more trouble than you can imagine because we are so set into thinking that we should hold onto the hurts of the past. We have somehow come to think that we must uncover causes of our hurts and wrong attitudes and there is in fact no Biblical support for such methods.

This is such an issue let's consider three summarized Biblical examples:

1) Joseph was mistreated by his brothers, then by Potiphar and his wife, and then by the butler. But no where do we see him going back to them and

having to forgive them or using them as an excuse. His revelation was simple – "you meant it for evil but at the same time God meant it for good." He did not go through inner healing for this revelation, but the testing of life burned out of him the bitterness of his own heart and he went on to live a healthy productive life saving two nations.

2) The children of Israel as slaves were delivered out of Egypt. Nowhere did God ever require them to forgive the Egyptians or pray for "healing" but rather they were continually tested to believe in God regardless of the circumstances. In fact, God expected them to move forward and forget Egypt – period. God actually provided at each stop on their journey from Egypt to the Promised Land an event that was designed for the people to discover more of God and His goodness, but they chose to look back and murmur over their difficulty.

God was trying to get them to quit looking back. He wanted them to experience a paradigm shift from a slave mentality to a ruling mentality in the Promised Land. Instead they chose to hold onto their bitterness and pain of the past. They refused God who wanted to enable them to move forward and as a result that generation failed to enjoy the Promise of God.

3) David was never told to forgive King Saul nor go back to reconcile with him. He honored him as king regardless of the cruelty he endured and went on with life until it was his day to reign as king. David did not need inner healing for how his brothers treated him when he came to challenge Goliath. He believed God, he trusted God, he worshipped God, and he served God – this is how he found his freedom from the past.

As I look back over my own church ministry I confess that I allowed a preoccupation with life's hurts take away from the power of the Gospel. There is nothing to gain by going back to the place that we think may have hurt us. When we see all that God has done for us and provided for us we will see that these things do not matter because "greater is He that is in me than he that is in the world." It is time to give forgiveness, drop our hold on our pains and hurts, and move forward.

Peter goes on to tell us to maintain that same attitude that newborn babies have – a focus on our next meal. The meal for us though is the word of God. Moses prophesied it, Jesus quoted it, and now Peter is testifying to it, "man shall not live by bread alone, but by every word that comes from the Father." In other words, let our appetites be minimized to set ourselves with a hunger for God.

Peter goes on with his message to challenge us to think of ourselves as spiritual. This is hard for us to grasp. We may have "spiritual moments" like when we get goose bumps in church during a song or sermon, but it is difficult for us to think of ourselves in a spiritual lifestyle. But Peter does not acknowledge our struggle with this life perspective. Rather he defines us as a new kind of people. New races if you will, people that are a chosen generation and in fact royal priests. Peter gives us the key to getting our lives into perspective. How do we tune in our antenna and receivers to the Holy Spirit? We must understand that after our salvation we no longer belong to this earth but we are foreigners and strangers. We have a heavenly citizenship and we belong above even while we are here on earth.

1 Peter 2:9, 10 *But you ARE a chosen generation, a royal priesthood, a holy nation, His own special people, that you may proclaim the praises of Him who called you out of darkness into His marvelous light; who once WERE not a people but ARE now the people of God, who had not obtained mercy but now have obtained mercy.*

This is the key to spiritual living. When we come into our faith of salvation we become a new kind of "people." Consider all the immigrants that have come from other nations to the USA. They had a language and culture and way of doing things. Those that have integrated here have taken on the culture of Americans. Their language changes, their diet changes, their way of doing things change. They take an oath to become an American citizen that pledges their allegiance to the American flag.

This is what Peter is urging all followers of Jesus Christ that have been born again by the Blood of the Lamb. Take on a new language of love and care for others. Change appetites so that we hunger for righteous living. Do things for the reasons and the way Jesus would do things. Pledge to serve the Lord with all your heart and all your strength and follow His ways.

In this chapter also Peter is driving home the fact that we are to be a praising people. We should show our praises, we should be different than those around us. When it says we are a "peculiar people" it literally means a "purchased people." In other words, the blood of Jesus paid for our sins and thereby bought us. In essence we have been bought and paid for. This goes against all political correctness and hearkens back to the days of slavery.

But there is a fine distinction here. We are not slaves by force but we are slaves willingly. In the Old Testament when someone had an obligation they could not pay they became slaves for seven years. There was a ring put in their left ear and they were duty bound to serve the master's requests for those seven years. At the end of the seven years they were free to go. But sometimes the slave liked working for the benevolent master so much that he made a free choice. He offered to continue to serve if the master accepted. Then there was a ritual that the ear ring would be removed from the left ear and put on the right ear.

Then every where the slave went all would know that he was a "bond slave" meaning that he served his master willingly and by choice. In today's vernacular we might call him a "free slave" – a slave by choice. This is what Peter is talking about. Our freedom has been purchased – we are no longer slaves to sin – and now we are free to choose to live and serve the King of kings and the Lord of lords.

Peter goes on to challenge us on a topic that is relevant as ever today. He challenges us to "abstain from fleshly lusts." All lust does is create a bigger war between our natural self and our spiritual self. This theme runs through both books that Peter wrote at the end of his life. In western society it seems we have relented in the war and assume that there is nothing we can do about the temptations that permeate the media. Regardless of the state of the battle within society we can and must win the battle within our own hearts and minds to abstain from fleshly lusts.

He then describes in summary form our relationship with the society around us. We are to maintain at all times a Holy lifestyle, we are pilgrims (literally strangers) on this earth, we should honor those in governmental authority, we should be good citizens, and we should do good works and be noted for such. He closes this brief description by telling us to honor others, love our fellow Christians, fear God, and honor the king (or top government officials). Peter is helping define what a Christian is within the context of any society.

At the end of 1 Peter 2 Peter brings forth a very important Biblical principle about the power of healing for Christians. Let's consider one key thought; how does healing work for us? The answer in God is always by faith. Again the arch enemy to our faith is doubt and unbelief. The natural human condition always whispers, "Is it God's will to heal you?" Your automated response should be a resounding – YES! Remember this, we are free slaves. We belong to God by choice and in faith. We operate by choice and we must make our choices known by our faith. We must come to the place that we believe that what He did for me and you has power and affect on what we experience as people.

By His stripes you WERE healed. Again this means that He does not need to do anything additional on our behalf for us to be healed. We need to learn to "tap into that provision" to find and apply His *completed* work for our present situation.

CHAPTER THREE
1 PETER 3

1 Peter 3:

Serving and Suffering for God's Glory

Wives, likewise, BE submissive to your own husbands, that even if some do not obey the word, they, without a word, may be won by the conduct of their wives, when they observe your chaste conduct ACCOMPANIED by fear. Do not let your adornment be MERELY outward— arranging the hair, wearing gold, or putting on FINE apparel— rather LET IT BE the hidden person of the heart, with the incorruptible BEAUTY of a gentle and quiet spirit, which is very precious in the sight of God. For in this manner, in former times, the holy women who trusted in God also adorned themselves, being submissive to their own husbands, as Sarah obeyed Abraham, calling him lord, whose daughters you are if you do good and are not afraid with any terror.

A Word to Husbands

Husbands, likewise, dwell with THEM with understanding, giving honor to the wife, as to the weaker vessel, and as BEING heirs together of the grace of life, that your prayers may not be hindered.

Called to Blessing

Finally, all OF YOU BE of one mind, having compassion for one another; love as brothers, BE tenderhearted, BE courteous; not returning evil for evil or reviling for reviling, but on the contrary blessing, knowing that you were called to this, that you may inherit a blessing. For

"HE WHO WOULD LOVE LIFE AND SEE GOOD DAYS,

LET HIM REFRAIN HIS TONGUE FROM EVIL, AND HIS LIPS FROM SPEAKING DECEIT.

LET HIM TURN AWAY FROM EVIL AND DO GOOD; LET HIM SEEK PEACE AND PURSUE IT.

FOR THE EYES OF THE LORD ARE ON THE RIGHTEOUS,

AND HIS EARS ARE OPEN TO THEIR PRAYERS;

BUT THE FACE OF THE LORD IS AGAINST THOSE WHO DO EVIL."

Suffering for Right and Wrong

And who IS he who will harm you if you become followers of what is good? But even if you should suffer for righteousness' sake, YOU ARE blessed. "AND DO NOT BE AFRAID OF THEIR THREATS, NOR BE TROUBLED." But sanctify the Lord God in your hearts, and always BE ready to GIVE a defense to everyone who asks you a reason for the hope that is in you, with meekness and fear; having a good conscience, that when they defame you as evildoers, those who revile your good conduct in Christ may be ashamed. For IT IS better, if it is the will of God, to suffer for doing good than for doing evil.

Christ's Suffering and Ours

For Christ also suffered once for sins, the just for the unjust, that He might bring us to God, being put to death in the flesh but made alive by the Spirit, by whom also He went and preached to the spirits in prison, who formerly were disobedient, when once the Divine longsuffering waited in the days of Noah, while THE ark was being prepared, in which a few, that is, eight souls, were saved through water. There is also an antitype which now saves us—baptism (not the removal of the filth of the flesh, but the answer of a good conscience toward God), through the resurrection of Jesus Christ, who has gone into heaven and is at the right hand of God, angels and authorities and powers having been made subject to Him.

Here Peter gives us a very **politically incorrect** message to Christian women. He challenges **women to "subject" themselves** – note, **not let husband *subjugate*** them – but an act out of their own heart. He goes on to tell them the inner person is much more important than how they look on the outside. If their husband is unsaved, they are told the way to win them to Christ is by a Holy lifestyle.

It is interesting to note that even in the early church often the wife was saved before the husband and Peter is giving advice on how the woman should help win the husband. It will be her manner of living pure and righteous before her husband while choosing to submit herself or deferring to him.

Submission is not like being a door mat doing whatever the husband wants to do and especially not doing what is evil. Every woman knows that she has great power in appeal and influence to her husband. Every wife needs to be taught how to gain and use this power.

God says something here through Peter that we have certainly lost in our western culture. Women are encouraged to have a *"meek and quiet spirit."* Contrariwise in our culture women are told to stand up and take their "rightful" place. This conflict should be no surprise since we are talking about two different belief systems. In the world women are told in essence that it is not fair to be second.

But notice what God says here in verse four, He recognizes that this kind of woman is paying a great price! When God recognizes a woman's willingness to pay the price to please Him (not so much just trying to please her husband), He takes note and He assumes more responsibility in covering (or protecting) this kind of woman. He goes on to say that the only way a woman does this is if she "trusts in God" like Sarah of old. So wives are given a special status when their trust in Him is manifested in a meek and quiet spirit.

We have also lost sight of the husband's leadership role. The man should fulfill the leadership role – not because a woman can't – but because this was the design of God. A house divided will fall. In America they fall over fifty percent of the time and primarily because they struggle with two heads. There is a legitimate argument that the men of this generation are abdicating their leadership role.

Leadership includes collaboration and working together, not one lording it over the other. A wise woman will fulfill her role of help mate and support and use her position to influence her husband to make good decisions. The husband will learn how to operate in the leadership role when he does not have to fight for it over every household decision and when he learns how to tap into the gifting that his wife brings to the relationship.

Peter then goes on to tell the man how he should understand his role as the husband. **The man is to honor his wife, treat her with equality, and if he mistreats her his prayers will be hindered.** Please see the significance of this phrase in the sentence. Your prayers will be hindered! In other words God says He will close His ears to your prayers if you mistreat your wife. Notice something else significant here. He promises blessing to the wife if she will fulfill her role.

He promises withholding if the husband does not fulfill his role.

When a husband "honors" his wife it means that he demonstrates how valuable she is by treating her with respect, treating her as if she were significant and important to him and to the family and friends. A wise man and a man of God will recognize that it is important to get agreement with his wife on all major decisions that affect the family.

The Bible says that when a man and a woman get married that the two become one. This is a miracle because in marriage they no longer are two individuals but merged into one. This is not a fifty-fifty proposition. This is where two parties give up their independence and become interdependent. This means there is a total reliance and commitment to one another. This relationship is not a place for manipulation or control. It is a place of mutual deferment and with a spirit of cooperation and giving and yielding to one another.

If each party would learn how to successfully fulfill their individual role as laid out by Peter here the marriage bond would be unbreakable. All too often we see each party preoccupied trying to get the other party to change in how they do things. It takes a while to learn that you cannot change someone else. The only person I can change is myself!

Then Peter goes on with the challenge to all believers. He tells us we are to discover how to get along with each other. Our relationships should include an intentional effort to find out how to live in agreement, how to have compassion, and how to love one another.

Again as we look back over Peter's experience we see the struggle he endured with getting along with others. He asked Jesus, "How many times do I have to forgive others?" In essence telling us he was pretty frustrated at the time with his brethren being at odds with him. Jesus of course said to forgive seventy times seven per day, meaning we do not have a right to hold our brethren hostage to what mistakes they may have made.

But Peter at the same time here is driving home the value of being of one mind. This principle seems to be totally lost on the western church. After all, we want to have our own mind about things and claim we have a right to do so! But Peter is telling us, just as he spoke of marriage harmony, he is speaking of broader horizontal relationships. In these relationships there is a higher place of harmony and that place is where we find "one mind together."

He makes the point that the key to finding one mind is to be focused on having compassion on others and do this as a group. And he goes on to say that we should focus on "doing good." The idea is that rather than sitting around thinking of shortcomings of others over past things that we as a group look forward to finding out how we can look ahead together and do good things together.

And again in this chapter Peter mentions that if you suffer in the doing of good, that's ok! We should be always ready to share our faith – be ready to give reason **why we believe – not why they should believe**. There is a big difference here. So often our testimony is built on the premise that we are trying to get others to believe.

We try to get the plan of salvation into four or five "easy steps." But the world is looking at us and needs to hear how God worked in our heart and lives. Our responsibility is to share what God has done in and for us. No one can argue with that. They can argue with our ideas or refuse what we tell them that God wants to do in their lives.

Peter then references Noah and that God was waiting for about one hundred and twenty years during the building of the ark to see who would receive the message of hope and life. Sadly only eight people were saved by the preaching of Noah and by water when the earth was judged by the flood.

But now the resurrection of Jesus provides for us all. Our sins can no longer separate us from Him because Jesus paid for all our sins. Jesus is at the right hand of God and all power is His. Our conscience is no longer able to hold us prisoner because of the price He paid for us. The promise to all of us is complete reconciliation with God.

We must seek to show others how this reconciliation works and how it worked for us.

CHAPTER FOUR
1 PETER 4

1 Peter 4: The challenge to live in the spiritual dimension-it includes suffering

Christ's Example to Be Followed

Therefore, since Christ suffered for us in the flesh, arm yourselves also with the same mind, for he who has suffered in the flesh has ceased from sin, that he no longer should live the rest of HIS time in the flesh for the lusts of men, but for the will of God. For we HAVE SPENT enough of our past lifetime in doing the will of the Gentiles—when we walked in lewdness, lusts, drunkenness, revelries, drinking parties, and abominable idolatries. 4 In regard to these, they think it strange that you do not run with THEM in the same flood of dissipation, speaking evil of YOU. They will give an account to Him who is ready to judge the living and the dead. For this reason the gospel was preached also to those who are dead, that they might be judged according to men in the flesh, but live according to God in the spirit.

Serving for God's Glory

But the end of all things is at hand; therefore be serious and watchful in your prayers. And above all things have fervent love for one another, for "LOVE WILL COVER A MULTITUDE OF SINS." BE hospitable to one another without grumbling. As each one has received a gift, minister it to one another, as good stewards of the manifold grace of God. If anyone speaks, LET HIM SPEAK as the oracles of God. If anyone ministers, LET HIM DO IT as with the ability which God supplies, that in all things God may be glorified through Jesus Christ, to whom belong the glory and the dominion forever and ever. Amen.

Suffering for God's Glory

Beloved, do not think it strange concerning the fiery trial which is to try you, as though some strange thing happened to you; but rejoice to the extent that you partake of Christ's sufferings, that when His glory is revealed, you may also be glad with exceeding joy. If you are reproached for the name of Christ, blessed ARE YOU, for the Spirit of glory and of God rests upon you. On their part He is blasphemed, but on your part He is glorified. But let none of you suffer as a murderer, a thief, an evildoer, or as a busybody in other people's matters. Yet if ANYONE SUFFERS as a Christian, let him not be ashamed, but let him glorify God in this matter.

For the time HAS COME for judgment to begin at the house of God; and if IT BEGINS with us first, what will BE the end of those who do not obey the gospel of God? Now

"IF THE RIGHTEOUS ONE IS SCARCELY SAVED,

WHERE WILL THE UNGODLY AND THE SINNER APPEAR?"

Therefore let those who suffer according to the will of God commit their souls TO HIM in doing good, as to a faithful Creator.

Peter dwells again on the suffering example of Christ – and challenges us that we should have the same mindset as Christ – a willingness to suffer in the flesh for others. Again he reiterates that we should no longer live in the sins of the flesh, but we should live in the will of God.

He spells out many of these sins and tells us that we must give account for our actions. We should live temperate lives, live as if the end is near, he then again tells us to love each other. In fact we should read these verses carefully. Peter is driving the point home, he is relentless, and he is preaching and pleading with us to put away the demands of the flesh. He goes so far as to say that suffering will do us good for getting rid of the desire for sins.

As mentioned above in our possible death bed mindset the things of this earth grow faintly dim quickly under these circumstances. Accountability moves to the top of the list, and our feelings get quickly reordered. That our life would center on what is important to God and not on what is actually meaningless in our current physical environment should be the perspective for all of us to live under.

A key purpose of the preaching of the gospel is to help us turn from the ways of evil. Turn from the ways of evil thinking, excesses of the flesh, and the desires to do so. Peter reminds us that the judgment day is close at hand and that we should live according to the spirit, staying sober and in prayer.

He then goes on to tell us that whatever gift we have we should share and give to our brethren. He then challenges us that whatever gifting we have, we should use it to the maximum, reminding us of the parable of the talents. Use who we are or what we have to the glory of God. This comes as we give to others.

Remember the teaching of Jesus about the talents. To the one who had five talents, by the time the master returned he produced ten talents to give to the master. The concept is clear and obvious. Whatever we each have been given Christ expects us to produce and be ready to give back not only what we have been given but more. He expects us to take responsibility and take on the effort required to multiply what we have been given.

Unfortunately there is a principle by experience that seems to hold true. Take a look around your own church and see if it is true or not. The principle is that twenty percent of the people do eighty percent of the work. Somewhere along the generations of the church the idea that church is about us took hold. We enjoy programs and studies that we like and that please us. Our meetings are for the purpose of pleasing us.

What would happen if churches everywhere suddenly said the meetings are to save the lost, heal the brokenhearted, preach deliverance to the captives, recover sight for the blind and set at liberty them that are bruised? (Luke 4:18)

After John the Baptist was in jail and facing death he sent two of his disciples to ask Jesus are you the one we are looking for or not? We can read into this that John was frustrated because he was a Kingdom preacher and wondered why Jesus was taking so long to bring forth the Kingdom of God to earth. Well, here is Jesus' response:

Luke 7:22, 23 *Jesus answered and said to them, "Go and tell John the things you have seen and heard: that THE blind see, THE lame walk, THE lepers are cleansed, THE deaf hear, THE dead are raised, THE poor have the gospel preached to them. And blessed is HE who is not offended because of Me."*

John wanted a reality check and Jesus gave him one. It was not time for the Kingdom but these activities were proof that what Jesus was doing evidenced that He was truly the Sent One.

Is it time to take a reality check of the church of Jesus Christ here and now in America? What proof do we have to offer that we are real? Are the things Jesus offered as proof being done by us?

Is our church enabling the blind to see, the lame to walk, the lepers cleansed, the deaf hearing, and the dead raised up? Are we preaching to the poor? If our answer is these things don't happen anymore – BZZZZ – that is the bell going off for the wrong answer! Did not Jesus say, "Greater things will you do because I go to My Father in heaven?"

Peter, as should we, discovered how to tap into the enablements of heaven to be used here on earth. Maybe we need to recover these enablements and apply them to our gifts and go from there.

Now in this chapter Peter goes right back into the suffering and fire of testing that comes into our lives. By the way suffering for doing wrong is not what is being talked about here. He goes on that it is a privilege to suffer for the cause of Christ. And if you suffer in this cause – trust him for the keeping of your soul.

Peter closes this chapter by informing us that judgment will come and that it will begin in the house of the Lord. Peter witnessed judgment on Ananias and Sapphira and is warning the church there is more to come. But the Jesus will keep us!

CHAPTER FIVE
1 PETER 5

Shepherd the Flock - Instructions and Final Greeting

The elders who are among you I exhort, I who am a fellow elder and a witness of the sufferings of Christ, and also a partaker of the glory that will be revealed: Shepherd the flock of God which is among you, serving as overseers, not by compulsion but willingly, not for dishonest gain but eagerly; nor as being lords over those entrusted to you, but being examples to the flock; and when the Chief Shepherd appears, you will receive the crown of glory that does not fade away.

Submit to God, Resist the Devil

Likewise you younger people, submit yourselves to YOUR elders. Yes, all of YOU be submissive to one another, and be clothed with humility, for

"GOD RESISTS THE PROUD,

BUT GIVES GRACE TO THE HUMBLE."

Therefore humble yourselves under the mighty hand of God, that He may exalt you in due time, 7 casting all your care upon Him, for He cares for you.

Be sober, be vigilant; because your adversary the devil walks about like a roaring lion, seeking whom he may devour. Resist him, steadfast in the faith, knowing that the same sufferings are experienced by your brotherhood in the world. But may the God of all grace, who called us to His eternal glory by Christ Jesus, after you have suffered a while, perfect, establish, strengthen, and settle YOU. To Him BE the glory and the dominion forever and ever. Amen.

Farewell and Peace

By Silvanus, our faithful brother as I consider him, I have written to you briefly, exhorting and testifying that this is the true grace of God in which you stand. She who is in Babylon, elect together with YOU, greets you; and SO DOES Mark my son. Greet one another with a kiss of love.

Peace to you all who are in Christ Jesus. Amen.

Now Peter closes his first epistle with a word to the leaders of the church. Interestingly he challenges the leaders to "feed the flock." The same words Jesus spoke to Peter on the shores of Galilee. Now he passes on to others. This is just the way it is – what Jesus gives us we are to give to others. The leaders are to "feed the flock," not for personal gain, not by force or control, but with a willing heart. Peter promises that when the Chief Shepherd returns it will be with eternal rewards to those who do it.

Peter proved to the church that he truly loved Jesus. The proof was in the care and feeding of the flock of God. Our motivation for using our gifting in the church must be because we love Jesus. If we are motivated for any other reason we will miss the point that the Church is about Jesus and for Jesus. He gave his life for the Church and we must foster these concepts and teach these principles so that others may live for Christ.

Let us take note of what Peter does not tell shepherds of local churches to do. He does not tell them to have programs and events that are currently popular. He does not tell them to have the latest and greatest teachings that everyone wants to hear. He does not tell them to build churches with crystal chandcliers and padded pews. He does not tell them to learn how to be great orators. He does not tell them how many elders to have or how many deacons. He does not tell them how long the service should be. He merely tells them what Jesus told him.

He tells them to "feed the flock."

This is what the word **feed means**:

1) to feed, to tend a flock, keep sheep **a)** to rule, govern

2) to furnish pasture for food

3) to nourish

4) to cherish one's body, to serve the body

5) to supply the requisites for the soul's need

Further note Peter declares what so many of us miss when it comes to life in church. He does not say feed them what they want or how they want it. So many today think they can dictate how, when, and what they "feed on" in church. The implication from Peter here is that it is up to the shepherd. Furthermore then, the implication is that if you find a church that you believe God has for you, then don't try to change how your fed. It is after all your free choice to choose BUT you better do so under the inspiration of the Holy Spirit.

Notice an important word in **verse 10: AFTER you have suffered.** Peter hammers home the fact that suffering will be a part of our living experience as a Christian on this earth.

But, take comfort in the fact there is a time when suffering is done, it is over with! Notice what God will do in us and for us after our time of suffering:

1) He will *perfect or complete us*, making us what we were intended to be! The good news about this is that life is a journey. Sometimes it is difficult to see where we are going or what we are going to do when we get there. But God will put the finishing touches on us. He has good intentions for each individual person ever born. He always sees what they were intended to be and do in this life. Consider what happened to Joseph after he suffered unfairly in prison those twelve years, God used that fire to burn off the bitterness and to bring Joseph to the place of

completion. Furthermore, in the spirit of this perfection done by God, we will be repaired. Whatever has been torn from us will be restored and mended.

We will be equipped with whatever we need to accomplish that which God has chosen us for. This promise by God is a word of comfort to all hearts that are in the midst of suffering. And surly the suffering prophesied to come will require the Church to understand these truths personally.

2) He will **establish us**, meaning that we will have a foundation and can't be knocked off. He will "set us" like set in stone! We will be firm and sure. We will be strengthened and we will be constant and fixed in direction. We will be stable. Think about it. This is what God will do in us and for us and we will no longer live life on a roller coaster. There comes a day when we can live our lives in a steady fashion. No longer subject to which way the wind is blowing.

3) He will **strengthen us**. We will be stronger to push through on our own; we are built for the battle and strengthened to fight another day. This strengthening is in the soul realm. We will not be up and down in our own minds. We will have new confidence in ourselves and in our own well being. We will not be knocked over by everything contrary that comes along. We will be able to take a punch and give one back!

4) He will *settle us*. This is a place of contentment
where we know that we know that we are His and that
nothing and no one can separate us from His love. When
we are settled the wondering what is next is no longer a
thought or a fear. We are people that are built upon the
Rock and that Rock is Christ Jesus. When the rains
come and the wind blows and beats upon us we will not
fall for we are founded upon that Rock.

Peter then challenges the leaders to think in terms of
humility and mutual submission to one another.
Especially the younger should just submit themselves to
the older. Humility is the hall mark of leadership in the
faith. Humility is a life attitude. It is developed over
time. It takes confidence to be humble. Humility comes
to those with good self esteem. When a leader is humble
he thinks of himself in lowliness of mind, modestly, and
not of great significance. The opposite is arrogance and
pride. If we are proud actually God will resist us, but if
we are humble God will grant us grace – or enablement
– to feed the flock and give proper oversight to the
church.

Peter admonishes the leaders to cast their cares on Him.
This is a place of comfort to leaders. When you cast
your cares it means that you no longer bear the burden of
those things you have need of. Rather you are trusting
God for your needs.

Peter warns the leaders to be sober in life. Be careful
and aware that there is an enemy afoot. He is looking
for who he can pick off. He is hunting for leaders that

are vulnerable and leaders must be vigilant and careful not to be found in vulnerable situations. The admonition is to resist the devil and all his temptations.

A leader in the church needs a special daily sensitivity to the inspiration of the Holy Spirit. The word inspiration means just that, "breathed into." The people will always make their demands. People will clamor to hear the teachings that are pleasing to their ears. But the Lord is looking for those leaders who will worship the Lord in Spirit and in Truth. These will then plug into God and will know where to take the people, what to lead the people to do, and what to say to the people.

Peter does not tell the leaders any other "tricks of the trade." It is a transparent, humble, and obedient leader that is called to "feed My sheep!"

CHAPTER SIX
2 PETER 1

2 Peter 1: Greeting the Faithful - Grow in Christian Character

Simon Peter, a bondservant and apostle of Jesus Christ,

To those who have obtained like precious faith with us by the righteousness of our God and Savior Jesus Christ:

Grace and peace be multiplied to you in the knowledge of God and of Jesus our Lord, as His divine power has given to us all things that PERTAIN to life and godliness, through the knowledge of Him who called us by glory and virtue, by which have been given to us exceedingly great and precious promises, that through these you may be partakers of the divine nature, having escaped the corruption THAT IS in the world through lust.

Fruitful Growth in the Faith

*But also for this very reason, giving all diligence, add to your **faith** virtue, to **virtue** knowledge, to **knowledge** self-control, to **self-control** perseverance, to **perseverance** godliness, to **godliness** brotherly kindness, and to **brotherly kindness love.** For if these things are yours and abound, YOU will be neither barren nor unfruitful in the knowledge of our Lord Jesus Christ. For he who* *lacks these things is shortsighted, even to blindness, and has forgotten that he was cleansed from his old sins.*

Therefore, brethren, be even more diligent to make your call and election sure, for if you do these things you will never stumble; for so an entrance will be supplied to you abundantly into the everlasting kingdom of our Lord and Savior Jesus Christ.

Peter's Approaching Death

For this reason I will not be negligent to remind you always of these things, though you know and are established in the present truth. Yes, I think it is right, as long as I am in this tent, to stir you up by reminding YOU, knowing that shortly I MUST put off my tent, just as our Lord Jesus Christ showed me. Moreover I will be careful to ensure that you always have a reminder of these things after my decease.

The Trustworthy Prophetic Word

For we did not follow cunningly devised fables when we made known to you the power and coming of our Lord Jesus Christ, but were eyewitnesses of His majesty. For He received from God the Father honor and glory when such a voice came to Him from the Excellent Glory: "This is My beloved Son, in whom I am well pleased." And we heard this voice which came from heaven when we were with Him on the holy mountain.

And so we have the prophetic word confirmed, which you do well to heed as a light that shines in a dark place, until the day dawns and the morning star rises in your hearts; knowing this first, that no prophecy of Scripture is of any private interpretation, for prophecy never came by the will of man, but holy men of God spoke AS THEY WERE moved by the Holy Spirit.

Peter already observed that corrupt teachers and false doctrine was moving throughout the church and he began to warn believers to be alert.

Peter wrote this second book specifically to fellow believers. He rehearses the fact that Divine Power is at work in the life of each believer. Now wait a minute – read this last sentence again. Divine Power is at work in the life of each believer! The question for each of us is how and when is this power working in my life? What am I doing to cultivate this Divine Power? When was the last time I demonstrated this power at work in my life?

His power has been given to us to live in godliness, and it will enable us to partake of the Divine Nature and give us the power to overcome the corruption of this world through our own lust. Here is how it works. Peter gives us a ***Character Development Plan for Successful Christian Living*** on earth. If we will live our lives making a daily effort to pay attention to and consider how to improve each of the following character qualities we will live and demonstrate Divine Power;

Let's look at each of these character qualities and consider what it will take for us to grow in each quality:

FAITH

Faith is the conviction of the truth of anything, belief; in the New Testament of a conviction or belief respecting man's relationship to God and divine things, generally with the included idea of trust and holy fervor born of faith and joined with it.

Relating to God it is with the conviction that God exists, and is the creator and ruler of all things. Relating to Christ faith is the welcome conviction that Jesus is the Messiah and the bestower of salvation.

Faith is not some mysterious concept. Faith is the substance of things hoped for the evidence of things not seen. To every man has been given a measure of faith. So often the faith of people is denigrated by others as a weakness. In fact, faith is strength. In Christ our faith is based on who He is and what He does. The more we know and understand how Jesus thinks and acts and what motivates Him the more faith we will have.

The expression often currently quoted – "what would Jesus do?" – is only part of the equation. We must seek to understand Jesus and find out how He thinks and why He does the things He does. Paul said "let this mind be in you which is also in Christ." This means that it is possible to begin to think like Jesus thinks. In order for us to do that we must first spend time with Him. How do we do that? We read the red. Many Bibles have the words of Jesus written in red. We must study His words in the Bible and understand them. My pastor says you can't just read the Bible you have to read the Bible. We must read between the lines. We must think about how and why He says what He says and does what He does. We must pray and ask the Holy Spirit to guide us into all truth.

In the history of the NFL no one has ever just shown up on a Sunday and played the game without ever going to practice. To play at this level requires working out and studying film daily for months and years. In addition, it takes size and speed and ability. It takes proving yourself on lower levels like at high school and college. While it takes ability it also takes heart. I have seen a lot of players that did not have all the speed and size yet they played because they had the "heart" to play. On the other side I have seen many with all of the physical capabilities but could not make it because they did not have the heart to put their qualities on the line.

What is this heart that overcomes a lot of other short comings? It is the belief that you want to and can play, that you will do what it takes regardless of the cost. It is the commitment to hit and play your hardest regardless of the circumstances or the ability of your opponents.

Somehow we as Christians think we can show up on Sunday and play Christianity! Then we want to question Jesus why He did or didn't do something in our life that we expected or wanted. Somewhere along the way we have come to think we can read our Bible for a few minutes a month and then think we can understand who

Jesus is and how He thinks. By the way, man looks on the outward or appearance of other men, but God looks on the heart. He is looking for those imperfect souls who have a heart that seeks after Him.

If someone has cancer he doesn't go to a cardiac specialist. He goes to a cancer doctor and seeks out the specific doctor that has experience with the specific cancer that he has. Find the expert. Find the help you need from someone who knows the ins and outs of what your problem is. Who are these experts? They are the ones who have been immersed in the study of your problem. They have spent years and seen hundreds or thousands of other patients with similar problems. They have read all the books and kept up with the latest studies and tests in the lab.

It takes days and years and a lifetime to truly "know" Jesus.

Perhaps we suffer with such a shallow understanding of Jesus that our faith is too often based on presumption or myth.

Let's be clear. How do we build our faith? We build our faith on the word of God. Faith comes by hearing and hearing by the word of God. We build our faith by knowing Jesus inside and out. The word confirmed in the mouths of two or three witnesses is sure. We must be willing to clear out of our mind the five senses that generally rule our lives here on earth so that we are ruled by the Spirit of God. This life is not to be ruled by what we see and feel. Our five senses are wonderful for keeping us in touch with the world around us.

But it is by the Spirit of God that we keep in touch with the heavenly world. Since one of our basic prayers says "thy Kingdom come on earth as it is in heaven," we can bring heaven to earth.

This sounds presumptuous when it is in fact expected. We all too often are waiting for God to do things in our lives and on earth when in fact He is waiting for us to do them. Faith is an active source of proactive steps to be taken by Christians. We must lose all doubt and unbelief. These things are enemies to our faith. If you have some doubt and some faith – in reality you have no faith. ten parts faith and one part doubt equals no faith!

If you pray wondering whether God will intervene on your behalf – then He won't! This will upset the theology of some – but regardless it is true. If we pray "wondering" that means we are in doubt. If we pray questioning whether it is His will or not – again we are in doubt. When we take the time to know Him and when we know His word then we don't have to guess whether something we are praying about is in His will or not. We will have confidence and know the answer to that – before we pray.

It is important to consider the following scriptures, read them, pray them, until we "own" them. When we own them we can operate in the faith Jesus urges His followers to operate in:

Matt 14:31, 32 *And immediately Jesus stretched out HIS hand and caught him, and said to him, "O you of little faith, why did you doubt?" And when they got into the boat, the wind ceased.*

Matt 21:21 *So Jesus answered and said to them, "Assuredly, I say to you, if you have faith and do not doubt, you will not only do what was done to the fig tree, but also if you say to this mountain, 'Be removed and be cast into the sea,' it will be done. And whatever things you ask in prayer, believing, you will receive."*

Mark 11:22-24 *So Jesus answered and said to them, "Have faith in God. For assuredly, I say to you, whoever says to this mountain, 'Be removed and be cast into the sea,' and does not doubt in his heart, but believes that those things he says will be done, he will have whatever he says. Therefore I say to you, whatever things you ask when you pray, believe that you receive THEM, and you will have THEM.*

We see in the Mat 14 passage that Jesus first explained that doubt revealed "little" faith. In this case faith was disrupted by doubt and caused the loss of ability for Peter to keep walking on the water. Can we see that faith and doubt cannot coexist in the same mind at the same time over the same issue?

The Mat 21 passage and the Mark 11 passage are talking about the same time. We often read this and jump to the conclusion that we can pass it off because it talks about moving mountains. Moving mountains has never been recorded as having been done as the result of someone praying. So we dismiss the whole passage.

Obviously the passage is not talking about Mt. Everest or Mt. Kilimanjaro. We all face our mountains of problems or bills. We get nervous reading these kinds of passages instead of getting excited about them and trying to discover how we can experience them for ourselves.

In this passage we are finding out that what we say has power. The key to this power is that we must not have doubt in our heart. Rather we must believe – have faith. We must believe that what we say will truly happen. If we do we shall have what we say! Just because these things have been abused does not mean they are not true. Just because people have said they believe but the evidence is that they do not believe in their heart – does not mean these words are not true. We must discover how this process works and not wallow around mired in doubting the power of this truth.

The father of faith is Abraham:

Romans 4:3-5 *For what does the Scripture say? "ABRAHAM BELIEVED GOD, AND IT WAS ACCOUNTED TO HIM FOR RIGHTEOUSNESS. Now to him who works, the wages are not counted as grace but as debt. But to him who does not work but believes on Him who justifies the ungodly, his faith is accounted for righteousness,*

<u>Romans 4:16</u> *Therefore it is of faith that it might be according to grace, so that the promise might be sure to all the seed, not only to those who are of the law, but also to those who are of the faith of Abraham, who is the father of us all*

Abraham was called by God to leave the land where he lived. To understand this we must realize that he lived and was rich and successful in a city that was the equivalent of New York City of our time. He was told that God would show him after he started packing and walking where he was going to end up. This was a remarkable event when you consider the world at that time. Abraham lived in the center of civilization and was told to head out to land unknown.

His faith was proved by his steps. Later he was promised an heir. Even though it took decades for him to receive this promise Abraham held on and believed. Then Abraham was told to take this son – his heir of promise – and sacrifice him on a mount that would be shown to him as he started walking. Abraham believed God,

<u>Hebrews 11:17-19</u> *By faith Abraham, when he was tested, offered up Isaac, and he who had received the promises offered up his only begotten SON, of whom it was said, "IN ISAAC YOUR SEED SHALL BE CALLED," concluding that God WAS able to raise HIM up, even from the dead, from which he also received him in a figurative sense.*

<u>Gal 3:6</u> *just as Abraham "believed God, and it was accounted to him for righteousness."*

<u>Gal 3:14</u> *that the blessing of Abraham might come upon the Gentiles in Christ Jesus, that we might receive the promise of the Spirit through faith.*

Obedience is a proof of faith. Walking without knowing where exactly you are going but believing you are following His direction, is evidence of faith. Faith is a journey for all of us. It is a life adventure. Let it start today. Study and come to understand every step taken by Abraham. Study and come to understand every step taken by Jesus. Record every step, take note and follow the path He has for your life.

Next Peter wrote that we should add something to our faith. He said to add virtue to our faith:

* FAITH

VIRTUE

Virtue means virtuous course of thought, feeling and action- moral goodness moral excellence, as modesty, purity

It is quite telling that Peter first adds virtue to our faith in the character development process. Let's ask ourselves why? This is a vital question when reading the Bible. You will discover that the best way to interpret the Bible is with the Bible. When you ask why you will find answers that will build your faith.
Why is virtue to be added to our faith? It must be important that faith remain pure. It is of paramount importance that our faith not be exercised to do evil. Our faith must be clothed in purity and moral goodness.

Our faith must carry with it right thinking. We cannot be the kind of people that go off half cocked just doing whatever we feel like doing. In our western culture deciding to remain pure must be a conscious committed decision. But the decision does not stop there. Living pure requires conscious decision making daily.

We must guard our hearts. We must guard our eyes. We must guard our minds. We must be most careful in what we allow our hearts to yearn for. We must be willing to close our eyes when temptation lures. We must not allow our minds to drift to the base things of life. Fantasy thinking of illicit behavior is harmful.

Yet you say no one is hurt. I would say yes you are hurt
if you let fantasy rob you of your personal purity. Jesus
said "he who looks on a woman to lust after her is an
adulterer." So it is not even the action it can be the
imagination that affects our virtue.

We cannot have ulterior motives in the use of our faith.
It cannot be for personal gain. Faith is based on the rules
of the Kingdom of God. Even while we are on earth it is
the Kingdom thinking and interpretation of events that
matter. A problem we all face is the preoccupation we
have with the world around us. It is amazing how often
the things of this world are in conflict with the things of
the Kingdom of God.

Phil 4:8 *Finally, brethren, whatever things are true,
whatever things are noble, whatever things are just,
whatever things are pure, whatever things are lovely,
whatever things are of good report, if there is any virtue
and if there is anything praiseworthy—meditate on these
things.*

Virtue carries with it the concept of purity
a) Pure from carnality, chaste, modest
b) Pure from every fault, immaculate
c) Clean

As we consider these words we must look at them
closely. We must consider the weight of the words, and
the power that they represent. This means that we must
translate these words into action. These are not merely
chosen because they rhyme or that they sound good.

Virtue must consciously be a part of our lives. We must work virtue into our actions both public and private.

We have been laboring under the delusion that private actions that don't hurt anyone else are no big deal. This rationalization cannot rule our lives. First of all let us realize that impure thoughts and actions hurt us. We don't recognize it because the hurt is not apparent. It is not like a poke in the eye. It is more like we smoke cigarettes for twenty or thirty years and think we are enjoying it. Then "all of a sudden" we have heart problems, lung problems, and face a multiple of other health problems perhaps even facing death. Sin is like that. It tends toward death at all times. It may not seem like it and it may not feel like it, but one day you will wake up and "suddenly" be faced with the consequences.

A way to look at these things is like this. Life consists of how we see things, how others see things, and how God sees things. Obviously God's perspective is the only one that counts. The children of Israel spent forty years in the wilderness looking at their journey wondering why God wasn't preparing the table of food or the water BEFORE they came to the place in need. They never could "see things how God saw them." As a result that generation died in the wilderness. It is of paramount importance that we try to find out what God is doing in any situation. We must almost have an out of body experience, and look down at ourselves and see how God is seeing things. If He says the action we are contemplating is impure – then it is impure. Regardless of how innocuous an action or thought may seem, if God says it is wrong it is wrong.

Now the character qualities are growing beginning with

FAITH * VIRTUE

KNOWLEDGE

Knowledge- signifies in general, intelligence, understanding of Christian religion, the deeper more perfect and enlarged knowledge of this religion, such as belongs to the more advanced of things lawful and unlawful for Christians -- moral wisdom, such as is seen in right living

Proverbs 1:7 *The fear of the LORD is the beginning of knowledge, But fools despise wisdom and instruction.*

Proverbs 2:1-9 1 *My son, if you receive my words, And treasure my commands within you,*

So that you incline your ear to wisdom, AND apply your heart to understanding;

Yes, if you cry out for discernment, AND lift up your voice for understanding,

If you seek her as silver, And search for her as FOR hidden treasures;

Then you will understand the fear of the LORD, And find the knowledge of God.

For the LORD gives wisdom; From His mouth COME knowledge and understanding;

He stores up sound wisdom for the upright; HE IS a shield to those who walk uprightly;

He guards the paths of justice, And preserves the way of His saints.

Then you will understand righteousness and justice, Equity AND every good path.

We are not talking about knowledge from books. We are talking about knowledge from above. We must grasp that the Kingdom of God is at work on the earth. And our faith and virtue must operate in the knowledge of the Kingdom. All too often people assume certain things happen and that they are God's fault. Consider the example of a child suffering with cancer. How many times do we hear people question God either as to why He did it or why did He allow it. These questions come from lack of knowledge.

It is the "thief" who came to rob, kill, and destroy. That thief is the devil. And yet the ignorant want to blame God. This gives them an excuse to not humble themselves and come to God. According to some research a significantly high percentage of people who claim they are a Christian do not even "believe" there is a devil. Why do they think that? It is because of ignorance. They "perish for lack of knowledge."

The Bible enables us to discover who God is and how God thinks. When we have a reverential fear of God and realize His pervasive will for this world we start to gain knowledge. When we begin to see that our life is not

about us but about Him we start to gain more
knowledge. God is love and His love is everlasting.

I am amazed how few people today study the Old
Testament. Consider these verses;

<u>1 Corinthians 10:1-11</u> *Moreover, brethren, I do not want*
you to be unaware that all our fathers were under the
cloud, all passed through the sea, all were baptized into
Moses in the cloud and in the sea, all ate the same
spiritual food, and all drank the same spiritual drink.

For they drank of that spiritual Rock that followed them,
and that Rock was Christ. But with most of them God
was not well pleased, for THEIR BODIES were
scattered in the wilderness.

*Now these **things became our examples**, to the intent*
that we should not lust after evil things as they also
lusted. And do not become idolaters as WERE some of
them. As it is written, "THE PEOPLE SAT DOWN TO
EAT AND DRINK, AND ROSE UP TO PLAY." Nor let
us commit sexual immorality, as some of them did, and
in one day twenty-three thousand fell; nor let us tempt
Christ, as some of them also tempted, and were
destroyed by serpents; nor complain, as some of them
also complained, and were destroyed by the
destroyer. Now all these things happened to them as
examples, and they were written for our admonition,
upon whom the ends of the ages have come.

So we see Paul wrote to the Corinthians rehearsing some of the bad decisions made by the children of Israel in the wilderness. He then goes on to tell us that these are examples and written for us so that we will not make the same kind of wrong decisions.

Now if we take this charge seriously that the children of Israel are examples for us, we then will start looking into the details of the journey they had in the wilderness.

What we learn for one thing is that God is involved with us and that we have an interactive relationship with Him. They looked at the journey from their own point of view and this was a tragic mistake. It will be tragic for us also if we look at our lives from only our own point of view expecting God to just eliminate our problems before we have any.

But this is not how God works with us. He sees us through the troubles of life. He will never leave us nor forsake us, but He expects us, that when we have tribulation that we should be of good cheer; for He has overcome the world for us.

Just think that when they came to the Red Sea with the Pharaoh coming up behind them, that they were filled with fear and dismay. From their perspective there was no way out. From God's perspective He sees that He can deliver them out of the roadblock at the mere sound of a word spoken. And He used Moses to speak that word of salvation.

Let's be clear, they did not want to have to face a
dilemma. They wanted these things taken care of before
they got there. But God was and is after something else.
He wants us to realize that regardless of the mess we are
facing, that we can trust Him and believe on Him that He
will be with us and show us the way THROUGH to
eventual victory. When we come to know the heart of
God we will realize that He is always thinking in terms
of the bigger picture for our lives. He wants to build
character and fortitude so that we can walk in the victory
ourselves.

Think of the other time when they were without water
for three days they started accusing God of wanting to
kill them in the wilderness. Rather than this bizarre
conclusion they should have focused in faith believing
that He would provide water somehow or some way for
them. Their accusations revealed a deep bitterness in
their soul left over from their slavery abuses and God
wanted to heal that bitterness and make life sweet for
them.

Hosea 4:6 *My people are destroyed for lack of
knowledge. Because you have rejected knowledge,
I also will reject you from being priest for Me;
Because you have forgotten the law of your God,
I also will forget your children.*

Also in the Old Testament we see in Hosea 4 above that a person that lacks the knowledge of God and how He works, thinks and acts - will get lost in this life. How many people have died before "their time?" How many of us have suffered needlessly because we exposed ourselves to the working of the enemy out of ignorance. Notice in this account it says they "rejected knowledge." This means that some have said I know there is a way of God but I want to go my own way. Therefore, as we will reject Him He will reject us. If we accept Him He will accept us.

Romans 1:28 *And even as they did not like to retain God in their knowledge, God gave them over to a debased mind, to do those things which are not fitting;*

We also see in Romans that the time comes when people that have rejected God and refuse to retain or continue on with God, that God gives them over to the evil thoughts they have been harboring in the place of their thoughts of God. This is the most frightful place a human could find themselves in this life.

Without God in our life we are lost. We must remember that God is faithful. God so loved the world that He gave His only begotten Son. When He gives up on us it is because we have rejected all expressions of His love and have made a conscious decision to reject Him at all times and regardless of His efforts to find us.

<u>2 Corinthians 10:5</u> *Casting down imaginations, and every high thing that exalts itself against the knowledge of God, and bringing into captivity every thought to the obedience of Christ*

Here we see that our fantasy life and our imaginations can get carried away. We can dream things up and claim them as real. Here we also see that each of us has the capability to bring our thoughts under control. We can decide what we think about and what we dream about. We must take responsibility for what goes on in the theater of our mind.

FAITH * VIRTUE * KNOWLEDGE

TEMPERANCE

- Self-control (the virtue of one who masters his desires and passions, esp. his sensual appetites)

This is a major theme in the epistles of Peter. He makes a point several times that we are to flee youthful lusts. With the accessibility to pornography, free on the internet, and with the culturally acceptable revealing dress code that begins at about age TEN and goes now days to grandma's age, the temptations before us all require a new strength and determination to gain control over our sensual appetites.

One of the true benefits of fasting is learning how to gain control over the basic needs of our body. Years ago there was a teacher who recommended fasting one day per week. After following this recommendation for months you will begin to see that you in fact do have control over the demands of the flesh.

Isaiah 58:6-11 *Is not this the fast that I have chosen? to loose the bands of wickedness, to undo the heavy burdens, and to let the oppressed go free, and that ye break every yoke? Is it not to deal thy bread to the hungry, and that thou bring the poor that are cast out to thy house? when thou seest the naked, that thou cover him; and that thou hide not thyself from thine own flesh? Then shall thy light break forth as the morning, and thine health shall spring forth speedily: and thy righteousness shall go before thee; the glory of the*

LORD shall be thy re reward. Then shalt thou call, and the LORD shall answer; thou shalt cry, and he shall say, Here I am. If thou take away from the midst of thee the yoke, the putting forth of the finger, and speaking vanity; And if thou draw out thy soul to the hungry, and satisfy the afflicted soul; then shall thy light rise in obscurity, and thy darkness be as the noonday: And the LORD shall guide thee continually, and satisfy thy soul in drought, and make fat thy bones: and thou shalt be like a watered garden, and like a spring of water, whose waters fail not.

There are promises of God when we fast following His guidelines. It is not to make a show of ourselves, bragging that we are going a few meals without food. But it is between us and God. He will set us free from those things that plague us. We will have to give to the less fortunate. We will find healing and our star will rise, meaning that we will have good fortune. Maybe best of all the promise is that the Lord will guide us continually and we will prosper.

The promises that go along with temperance are substantial. As a nation we have virtually given over to our lusts and our restraints are getting fewer and fewer. We are accepting activities today that we thought were sin just ten or fifteen years ago.

<u>Galatians 5:22-25</u> *But the fruit of the Spirit is love, joy, peace, longsuffering, kindness, goodness, faithfulness, gentleness, **self-control**. Against such there is no law. And **those WHO ARE Christ's have crucified the flesh with its passions and desires.** If we live in the Spirit, let us also walk in the Spirit.*

Look how the Apostle Paul sees this topic. When we walk in meekness and temperance there is not a law that is against such good behavior. In other words such a person is always in the right. Paul goes further and says that we can and should "crucify our flesh," in other words, die in our minds to the demands of the flesh. If you poke a dead man he does not react. You cannot tempt a dead man with anything!

Paul goes on to say we should live and walk in the Spirit. This means that we allow ourselves to be ruled and lead by the Spirit of God. It is possible that we can think in those terms and walk in those terms. We can consciously keep in step with the Spirit by considering that He is with us where ever we go and therefore we will limit some of the places we may go, and limit what we will do in other places. This ability to restrain ourselves comes when we have an awareness that He is with us.

* FAITH * VIRTUE

* KNOWLEDGE * TEMPERANCE

Now we add…

PATIENCE

- Steadfastness, constancy, endurance the characteristic
of a man who is not swerved from his deliberate purpose
and his loyalty to faith and piety by even the greatest
trials and sufferings

The first use of the word patience in the New Testament
is in the following verse:

Matthew 18:26 *The servant therefore fell down before
him, saying, 'Master, have patience with me, and I will
pay you all.'*

It is used in the sense of "I know I owe you money, and
please be patient, and I will pay you back." In other
words it will take me a while; I am not going to be able
to pay you quickly but I will pay you (although in this
case he ended up failing to pay).

In the second use of the word in the following verse we
also see the sense of time passing:

Luke 8:15 *But the ones that fell on the good ground are
those who, having heard the word with a noble and good
heart, keep it and bear fruit with patience.*

In this second use we get a good picture of what patience
requires. You plant seed, and it goes upon the good
ground, and then after a time, the plant grows and begins
to come out of the ground. Later, depending on the type

of plant comes forth the fruit. If we take an orange tree, for example, when we plant a seedling it can take as many as five years to grow edible fruit.

This is what our life is like in Christ. The seed is the word of God. We receive that word and believe it. Then that word begins to take root in our heart. It begins to grow and have effect on our thoughts and behavior. We begin to imitate the word of God. We begin to understand the principles and we begin to assimilate them into our lives. We begin to walk in the word and live according to the word. Then we begin to bear fruit. This means our life will reflect the impact that Jesus has had on us. When looked at by others they will judge us to be Christians.

Romans 5:3 *And not only that, but we also glory in tribulations, knowing that tribulation produces perseverance (or patience);*

Now this scripture has elicited many jokes among Christians over the years. Jokes have been made because we can all identify with the work of tribulation in our lives. The joke has been, "don't pray for patience because the Biblical source of patience is tribulation!"

It has been said that God may be late but He is always on time. It may seem late to us but in reality it is in His perfect timing. While we wait something happens in our soul.

The questions that burn in our heart somehow fade even when they are not directly answered. The things we worry about become less urgent with the passing of time. Sometimes we have been anxious about something that was not in our best interests and God knows it.

<u>Romans 15:5, 6</u> *Now may the God of patience and comfort grant you to be like-minded toward one another, according to Christ Jesus, that you may with one mind AND one mouth glorify the God and Father of our Lord Jesus Christ.*

When God identifies Himself with patience or that He is the God of patience this should be a comfort to us all. It means He patiently waits for us. He waits for us to respond to Him and His means of salvation. He waits by allowing the putting of things in our road to cause us to choose His way or not. If we think about it, without patience none of us would have a chance. As a result of His patience we likewise must learn patience.

As He has shown us patience we likewise should show one another patience.

During the waiting periods of life there comes a time when we drop our anxiety, we give up our control of how we want something to end, and we settle in to a place of trusting God for the outcome. Perhaps the greatest lesson of patience is when we learn to trust in God – no matter what we see or feel. We believe that we can count on God that no matter the outcome we will be all right. We are at peace that things will be all right.

One time I was in one of those waiting situations and a
friend said, "Remember, they can beat you but they can't
eat you!" The point being that most tribulations in life
are not about life and death but whether we think we will
like the outcome or not. I can testify that some of the
outcomes I thought I would dread actually worked
together for good in my life.

* FAITH * VIRTUE * KNOWLEDGE

* TEMPERANCE * PATIENCE

Now we add….

GODLINESS

- Reverence, respect - piety towards God

For some reason we have come to think that godliness has to do with how good we are. We seem to think it is about whether we are acting like God. The sense of this word though runs deeper than our behavior. It goes to our attitude. It goes to the motivations of our hearts.

Godliness has more of this sense; when we think about God we are filled with respect. We are in awe of His goodness and love. We think of ourselves at these same moments as humble before Him. We dare not make claims of how good we are. We realize in these moments that God is everything and we are only what He makes of us. When we have true reverence of God we will walk carefully. We will be cautious of our words and actions.

Our motivation to do good is not an effort to achieve something. Our motivation is out of respect for Him. Rather than trying to gain recognition we seek to honor Him. In other words, we want to do good to please God because we have such reverential awe toward Him and toward who He is.

It is vital that the world around us see Him in us. We are to be Jesus in the flesh to our generation. The cliché is true; our actions speak of our attitude toward Him much louder than our words. When we live our lives in front of those around us, each and every one of them should be aware, by our actions, that we have an awe and respect toward God. They should see that our reverence motivates us to love God, love our neighbor, and love our enemies.

People will know us not after our flesh but after our spirit. They will testify that Jesus must be real for they can see by our actions that we have a reverential awe that is so great and honoring of God that they too will want to know him.

1 Timothy 4:7-10 *But reject profane and old wives' fables, and* **exercise yourself toward godliness**. *For bodily exercise profits a little, but godliness is profitable for all things, having promise of the life that now is and of that which is to come. This IS a faithful saying and worthy of all acceptance. For to this END we both labor and suffer reproach, because we trust in the living God, who is THE Savior of all men, especially of those who believe.*

Here Paul is telling his (spiritual) son Timothy, (his protégé), don't let your church get into silly philosophizing and empty psychobabble (which the church is doing in this generation), and start walking out your life in godliness. He goes on with a good current message the church needs to hear, bodily exercise will not mean a whole lot but godliness will always return a profit.

He is assuring Timothy that everyone should accept the responsibility to get to what is important in life and, at the same time, will give God a return on His investment in us. Live a life in godliness – in reverential awe and respect for God.

1 Timothy 6:3-7 *If anyone teaches otherwise and does not consent to wholesome words, EVEN the words of our Lord Jesus Christ, and to the doctrine which accords with godliness, he is proud, knowing nothing, but is obsessed with disputes and arguments over words, from which come envy, strife, reviling, evil suspicions, useless wranglings of men of corrupt minds and destitute of the truth, who suppose that godliness is a MEANS OF gain. From such withdraw yourself.*

Now godliness with contentment is great gain. For we brought nothing into THIS world, AND IT IS certain we can carry nothing out.

Paul is going after his son in the faith and pounding into him and his church the understanding that our words and teachings and our relationships and discussion groups must be ruled by godliness. All other motives will come to nothing. He goes on saying that the doctrine of the church must be clothed in godliness. Stop all the arguing over philosophies that matter not.

Living in godliness and being content with all that you have will be to you as great gain. All the other things will not matter for when the time comes and we leave this life we take nothing with us to the next life. The only possessions we will have in heaven will be based on our actions here on earth. These actions can create crowns for us in heaven.

*FAITH * VIRTUE * KNOWLEDGE *

* TEMPERANCE * PATIENCE *

GODLINESS

Now we add…

BROTHERLY KINDNESS

- Love of brothers or sisters, brotherly love - the love which Christians cherish for each other as brethren

Brotherly kindness is a great phrase. When you love someone like a brother or sister it speaks of pure motive. It does not carry with it the sense that you seek any gain from this love. It is a filial love that implies care for the person who is the object of this love. There is no hidden agenda in brotherly love. We do not seek advantage over our brother. In fact, we are looking for his best interests in our dealings with him. In addition, there is no sexual motive in this kind of love.

The Greek word used here is Philadelphia – which is why they call Philadelphia, PA the "city of brotherly love." We care for our brothers and sisters in a way that implies a desire on our part to help them and support them. Whatever their need may be we hope to help. We will be there for them in times of sickness, through the trials and tribulations of life with support on whatever level they may need.

Luke 10:30-37 *Then Jesus answered and said: "A certain MAN went down from Jerusalem to Jericho, and fell among thieves, who stripped him of his clothing, wounded HIM, and departed, leaving HIM half dead. Now by chance a certain priest came down that road. And when he saw him, he passed by on the other side. Likewise a Levite, when he arrived at the place, came and looked, and passed by on the other side. But a certain Samaritan, as he journeyed, came where he was. And when he saw him, he had compassion. So he went to HIM and bandaged his wounds, pouring on oil and wine; and he set him on his own animal, brought him to an inn, and took care of him.*

On the next day, when he departed, he took out two denarii, gave THEM to the innkeeper, and said to him, 'Take care of him; and whatever more you spend, when I come again, I will repay you.' So which of these three do you think was neighbor to him who fell among the thieves?"

And he said, "He who showed mercy on him."Then Jesus said to him, "Go and do likewise.

We see in this familiar story the kind of care and provision for someone that Peter is talking about. The "good Samaritan" is interesting in the fact that the Samaritans and Jews had nothing to do with each other. Yet apparently a Jew fell into trouble and two Jews walked past him and ignored him.

Then along comes a Samaritan and he cares for him. Notice the Samaritan "had compassion" on him. This goes with the principle of "love your neighbor" in which your neighbor runs into trouble and you are in a position to help and you do so.

The concept of "caring" for someone carries with it some of these connotations. It will cost you something to care for others. It may be monetary, it will be time, it will cause some inconvenience to you, and it may even cost you a friend. How could it cost you a friend? If you spend time reaching out to others and caring for others inevitably someone close to you will be resentful "of all the time you waste on others." They also may become jealous of your time and care of others.

When we know someone to be a Christian there is after all an eternal connection. We are in fact brothers and sisters in Christ. Our bloodline changes from the natural to the spiritual. We share our heavenly Father. Christ is our elder Brother. You will find as you travel around the world that the bond of Christ is the strongest bond there is.

In the western church we often fall short in our practice of "brotherly kindness." It has been said that familiarity breeds contempt. Sometimes we judge others and put them in a box or stereo type them that we withhold kindness because of their faults that we claim to see. To deal with this issue I have found another perspective. As soon as I "see" the faults in others, I have learned that what I am judging in them must also be in me! This takes some of the edge off of my judgmentalism and leaves room for kindness.

Somewhere along the way, I was taught that the brother or sister in Christ that I had a problem with was standing in the door of opportunity for me. No matter what my issue with them was it could be overcome if I would find a find a way to serve them. Serving others is a high purpose in Christian living. When you serve someone instead of looking down at them you will be looking up at them. You will gain a new perspective and then you can realize that they are people just like you and I and they are just trying to get through life as best they can.

*FAITH *VIRTUE*KNOWLEDGE*

*TEMPERANCE*PATIENCE*

*GODLINESS *BROTHERLY KINDNESS*

Now we add…

CHARITY (LOVE)

-Affection, good will, love, benevolence, God's kind of love – agape (Greek)

<u>2 Peter 1:7</u> *to godliness (add) brotherly kindness, and to brotherly kindness(add) love.(charity)*

Love (charity) here is a special kind of love. It is the kind that builds up the person who is the object of the love. It never tears down; it is not oriented to any measure of harm or taking away from someone. This is God's kind of love. He loves us while we were yet sinners. His love is not based on our performance. His love is unconditional and is enduring.

His love is restorative. He always wants to pick us up if we have fallen. He wants to embrace us if we are lonely. He wants to touch us if we are stranded with no place to go. He wants to speak to us when we have no idea what to do next.

Love is so important that even if I as a person have all the gifts of the Holy Spirit, and have the money to help all those in need, but if I do not have love then all I have means nothing.

<u>1 Corinthians 13:4-8</u> *Love suffers long AND is kind; love does not envy; love does not parade itself, is not puffed up; does not behave rudely, does not seek its own, is not provoked, thinks no evil; does not rejoice in iniquity, but rejoices in the truth; bears all things, believes all things, hopes all things, endures all things.* ***Love never fails.***

Love will stick by no matter how long it takes. Love does not want what others have. Love does not make itself important. Love will not falter or fail. This is how they shall know you are Christians by the love you have one for another.

<u>1 Corinthians 13:13</u> *And now abide faith, hope, love, these three; but the greatest of these is love.*

So we see in the context of our character qualities, that Peter saved the best for last. Love, the agape kind of love, God's kind of love, is the quality that every Christian must develop and it must be present in word and action in all circumstances and at all times.

How can we possibly "develop" agape kind of love in our hearts for others?

<u>1 Corinthians 16:13, 14</u> *Watch, stand fast in the faith, be brave, be strong. Let all THAT you DO be done with love.*

<u>Colossians 3:12-15</u> *Therefore, as THE elect of God, holy and beloved, put on tender mercies, kindness, humility, meekness, longsuffering; bearing with one another, and forgiving one another, if anyone has a complaint against another; even as Christ forgave you, so you also MUST DO.* ***But above all these things put on love,*** *which is the bond of perfection. And* ***let the peace of God rule in your hearts,*** *to which also you were called in one body; and be thankful.*

This kind of expressed love must be practiced. In other words, I must begin to act like I love you and treat you as if I love you. Then I will find that love will grow in my heart for you. Paul told the Corinthians let everything you do be done with love as the motivating power.

He told the Colossians that it is of the utmost importance that you put on love. The sense here is like putting on a coat before going out into the cold. It is a conscious decision. We choose to love one another. It is not driven by emotions. It is driven out of that place in our soul that is our will. I choose to love you.

Notice that Paul tells the Colossians that this love you put on and walk in, is the thing that will bring you together with fellow believers. It is the quality that will bind your hearts together and bring completeness to your relationship. In fact this level of relationship with fellow believers will bring you to the higher place of moral and spiritual maturity and completeness.

Now let's take a look at the promises of the next verse:

2 Peter 1:8 *For if these things are yours and abound, you will be neither barren nor unfruitful in the knowledge of our Lord Jesus Christ.*

In verse 8 above we see Peter telling us how this **Character Development Plan** will enable us to accomplish all that we are called to do for the Kingdom of God. It promises that we will abound which has a sense of meaning that we will be productive in the Kingdom.

We will flourish and be filled with life and have life to give to others. In addition, we will be fruitful. Meaning that we will bear fruit or multiply into the lives of others what we have built in our own lives.

2 Peter 1:9, 10 *For he who lacks these things is shortsighted, even to blindness, and has forgotten that he was cleansed from his old sins.*

Therefore, brethren, be even more diligent to make your call and election sure, for if you do these things you will never stumble;

But notice in verse 9 is the foretelling of what will happen to us if we do not build the Character Development Plan in our lives. If we do not grow in the ways of Jesus in our life we will miss out in being all we can be in Christ Jesus. When we do not take the time to diligently implement the teaching of Jesus and His word in our life we will walk around wondering why things aren't going right for us. We will stay bogged down in our sins and our old ways of doing things. So our responsibility is clear we must implement the word of God into our behavior and into our thinking.

This teaching on character development is among the most important legacies of the Apostle Peter.

Let's pause and consider why this is so important. When the first seven deacons of the church were identified consider what qualities the leadership was looking for in these men:

Acts 6:2, 3 *Then the twelve summoned the multitude of the disciples and said, "It is not desirable that we should leave the word of God and serve tables. Therefore, brethren, seek out from among you seven men of GOOD reputation, full of the Holy Spirit and wisdom, whom we may appoint over this business;*

The qualifications for the first deacons of the church were:

1) Honest report – meaning men considered "good men."

2) Full of the Holy Ghost – meaning men baptized in the Holy Spirit

3) Men with wisdom – meaning men that seemed to make good decisions.

Curiously as time went on reputation and power and wisdom were found to not be enough of a reason to be selected as a deacon. The early church discovered as does the church of this day that gifting is not enough. We find many gifted that are immoral or careless or lack integrity.

Some twenty years after these first deacons were chosen we see the Apostle Paul update the qualifications necessary for selecting deacons:

I Timothy 3:8-13 *Likewise deacons MUST BE reverent, not double-tongued, not given to much wine, not greedy for money, holding the mystery of the faith with a pure conscience. But let these also first be tested; then let them serve as deacons, being FOUND blameless. Likewise, THEIR wives MUST BE reverent, not slanderers, temperate, faithful in all things. Let deacons be the husbands of one wife, ruling THEIR children and their own houses well.*

 For those who have served well as deacons obtain for themselves a good standing and great boldness in the faith which is in Christ Jesus.

We see here that Paul identifies further character qualities required for deacons to demonstrate prior to their selection to the office. The Pentecostal/ Charismatic arm of the church tends to focus on the gifting side of people for church office. The Evangelical arm tends to focus on the "honest report" side of people.

We must come to grips with these words of Peter. We must develop the character content of new believers. We must build **FAITH * VIRTUE * KNOWLEDGE * TEMPERANCE *PATIENCE * GODLINESS * BROTHERLY LOVE * LOVE (AGAPE)** in the lives of all that call upon the Name of Jesus. When should we start teaching these qualities? I am convinced that by age five is not too early. It needs to be a part of every curriculum for every age group!

Going back to our text notice here the emphasis on these the last words of Peter that he declares to the church for all days:

<u>2 Peter 1:14, 15</u> *knowing that shortly I MUST put off my tent, just as our Lord Jesus Christ showed me. Moreover I will be careful to ensure that you always have a reminder of these things after my decease.*

These two verses are very sobering to me. Peter is emphasizing the importance of content of character for all believers to go for. One of the greatest leaders in America of the 20th century – Martin Luther King Jr. – said that he looked for the day when men and women would be judged for the "content of their character" and not the color of their skin. I hope for the day when the church will likewise judge and appoint leaders in this fashion without regard to their gifting!

Our western lifestyle is oriented toward achievement. But consistency of achievement comes only with a foundation of Godly character qualities. It seems to be a lost art to build character qualities into our lives. To build virtue into our lives for example, it takes a conscience effort to be virtuous when we have, at every turn, the opportunity to do otherwise.

We need to keep in mind these qualities and practice them daily. It is the same as trying to learn any skill. A carpenter needs to apprentice with an experienced carpenter until he learns the skills of the trade. The church must provide a mentoring environment that will intentionally build these character qualities into the lives of the disciples.

If we work these things into our life experience then we will be bountiful in this life. If we don't practice these character qualities then we will be like those that have forgotten all that Jesus has done for us. On the contrary if we do practice these things, we will find our success and fulfillment in the Kingdom of God on this earth.

Notice his terminology here – he is saying for emphasis – before I die I want all the church to understand these few important things. Peter is using these last words to "stir up" the believers to live right in God's eyes. After it is all said and done this **life is not about** the great things we do for God. It **is not about** how big our church is or how many times we preach, or how many people we preach to, but rather here is Peter – one of the founding men of the early church, apprehends the truth that what counts is *how do we live for God*.

Toward the end of this chapter Peter reiterates that we are not following some philosophy or clever fables, but he tells us that he was an eye witness on the mount of transfiguration. He says that he was there when God the Father gave honor to His Son Jesus. He tells of the voice from the "excellent glory." Remember when Peter was on the mount with Jesus and wanted to build three tabernacles, that he knew there was great significance to the event.

But the significance was a testimony that Peter nearing his last breath was able to share for the church to savor for all of the church age. That it could take comfort in the eye witness of three men that Jesus was confirmed from heaven to be the Son of His Father! They heard the voice for themselves. As one of three witnesses it has been verified and the proof would hold up in court. Furthermore, the proof that Jesus was the Beloved Son of the Father is borne out by the willingness of Peter to die in defense of the Gospel.

He closes this chapter with the call to the importance of the prophetic. We have a sure word from God. It is not a guessing game. Jesus fulfilled in His first coming everything prophesied about Him. This adds to the credence that we can expect that everything prophesied about His second coming will also happen.

CHAPTER SEVEN
2 PETER 2

2 Peter 2: (Peter warns us about destructive doctrines as well as false teaching and false teachers)

*But there were also **false prophets** among the people, even as there will be **false teachers** among you, who will secretly bring in destructive heresies, even denying the Lord who bought them, AND bring on themselves swift destruction. And many will follow their destructive ways, because of whom the way of truth will be blasphemed. By covetousness they will exploit you with deceptive words; for a long time their judgment has not been idle, and their destruction does not slumber.*

Doom of False Teachers

For if God did not spare the angels who sinned, but cast THEM down to hell and delivered THEM into chains of darkness, to be reserved for judgment; and did not spare the ancient world, but saved Noah, ONE OF eight PEOPLE, a preacher of righteousness, bringing in the flood on the world of the ungodly; and turning the cities of Sodom and Gomorrah into ashes, condemned THEM to destruction, making THEM an example to those who afterward would live ungodly; and delivered righteous Lot, WHO WAS oppressed by the filthy conduct of the wicked (for that righteous man, dwelling among them, tormented HIS righteous soul from day to day by seeing and hearing THEIR lawless deeds)— THEN the Lord knows how to deliver the godly out of temptations and to reserve the unjust under punishment for the day of judgment, and especially those who walk according to the flesh in the lust of uncleanness and despise authority. THEY ARE presumptuous, self-willed. They are not afraid to speak evil of dignitaries, whereas angels, who are greater in power and might, do not bring a reviling accusation against them before the Lord.

Depravity of False Teachers

But these, like natural brute beasts made to be caught and destroyed, speak evil of the things they do not understand, and will utterly perish in their own corruption, AND will receive the wages of unrighteousness, AS those who count it pleasure to carouse in the daytime.

THEY ARE spots and blemishes, carousing in their own deceptions while they feast with you, having eyes full of adultery and that cannot cease from sin, enticing unstable souls. They have a heart trained in covetous practices, AND ARE accursed children. They have forsaken the right way and gone astray, following the way of Balaam the SON of Beor, who loved the wages of unrighteousness; but he was rebuked for his iniquity: a dumb donkey speaking with a man's voice restrained the madness of the prophet.

These are wells without water, clouds carried by a tempest, for whom is reserved the blackness of darkness forever.

Deceptions of False Teachers

For when they speak great swelling WORDS of emptiness, they allure through the lusts of the flesh, through lewdness, the ones who have actually escaped from those who live in error. While they promise them liberty, they themselves are slaves of corruption; for by whom a person is overcome, by him also he is brought into bondage.

For if, after they have escaped the pollutions of the world through the knowledge of the Lord and Savior Jesus Christ, they are again entangled in them and overcome, the latter end is worse for them than the beginning. For it would have been better for them not to have known the way of righteousness, than having known IT, to turn from the holy commandment delivered to them. But it has happened to them according to the true proverb: "A DOG RETURNS TO HIS OWN VOMIT," and, "a sow, having washed, to her wallowing in the mire."

Now Peter issues warnings that are to be warnings to the church in all ages. There will be false prophets, there will be false teachers, and there will be many people that will go off and follow them. Then Peter outlines the judgment of God throughout history. There were the angels that were judged and then cast out of heaven and put in chains unto the coming judgment day. The whole world was flooded in the days of Noah but that God saved Noah and those that were his. He judged the cities of Sodom and Gomorrah reducing them to ashes but saved Lot. He goes on to say that even in the middle of judgment and terror, that God knows how to save those that are His.

Peter then warns that the people with the following characteristics are most vulnerable to the judgment;

a) Those that walk "after the flesh" in their lust,

b) Those that despise government over them,

c) Those that are self willed,

d) And those that speak against those in authority.

All of these will utterly perish in their own corruption. Peter goes on to say that the following kind will receive the "reward of their unrighteousness;" partying during the day, deceivers of others, eyes full of adultery, those that lead astray the unstable, practice covetous dealings with others, and others that have forsaken the right way. While they speak great words of vanity, they draw others through the lust of the flesh, and that while they promise liberty they themselves are bound in sin.

Comparing Peter's writings with the Apostle Paul, the church today should understand their profound warning. Paul time after time warned *"be not deceived,"* meaning there are teachers and leaders teaching and leading people to follow them for gain. These teachers are very clever and can win many over by touching chords of lust within the hearts of their hearers.

Now Peter warns that *we cannot keep practicing sinful acts*. The point is that in spite of these two themes running through the church Patriarch's writings the church seems to ignore the fact that leading people away from the holiness of God and living away from the holiness of God will bring judgment and destruction to the participants. Even though they are Christians!

Peter challenges believers that if after they have come to the saving knowledge of Jesus Christ they forsake or turn away the end for them will be worse than if they had never known! For there is a reality that will come into play – for it will be revealed when they are as a dog that returns to his own vomit. But the Patriarch is telling us that in his long life he had seen it all. He was there for Ananias and Sapphira, he watched believers fall away down through the years, and in his last words he wants to urge the church don't let it happen to you.

Peter mentions historical judgment as an insight that judgment is part of the plan of God for earth:

- Angels that followed Satan – are in chains
- The world in time of Noah from the flood – all living souls died but 8 including Noah –
- Sodom and Gomorrah- 2 cities destroyed for failing to respond to God on their day of visitation.

Whether we want to argue end time theology or not – there is a coming judgment and we must be in right standing with God for His protection. Consider the

five foolish virgins: When they realized that they had
run out of oil for their lamps, they tried to get oil
from the five wise virgins. They were told you have
to go and buy your own oil.

Now consider the symbolism here. The oil represents in
most other Biblical references the Person of the Holy
Spirit. We know you can't "buy" the Holy Spirit. So
why were they told to go and buy their own oil? My
conclusion is this. I cannot buy the things of God or the
revelation of God. But when I receive Him and all that
He has done for me I then "buy into" the truth of the
Gospel and I take ownership of the fact that He saved me
and loves me.

The five foolish virgins evidently did not have personal
"buy in" to Jesus and when there came a knock at the
door the Bridegroom said, "I don't know you."

Matthew 25:11, 12 *"Afterward the other virgins came
also, saying, 'Lord, Lord, open to us!' But he answered
and said, 'Assuredly, I say to you, I do not know you.'*

There was also another time Jesus gave us this example
on the subject:

Matthew 7:20-23 *Therefore by their fruits you will know
them. "Not everyone who says to Me, 'Lord, Lord,' shall
enter the kingdom of heaven, but he who does the will of
My Father in heaven. Many will say to Me in that day,
'Lord, Lord, have we not prophesied in Your name, cast
out demons in Your name, and done many wonders in*

Your name?' And then I will declare to them, 'I never knew you; depart from Me, you who practice lawlessness!'

The judgment of the Lord is a frightful thing. Evidently there will be those that "ASSUME THEY ARE IN THE FAITH" when in fact they are not in the faith. Once someone told me their father got last rites before he died so he was in heaven. I knew his father and in fact knew he prayed the prayer of repentance and faith – because he did it in my presence. And I told the son last rites don't determine in and of itself whether we qualify for heaven – it is repentance and confession of faith and fruit of that reality that must be in evidence in the life of every believer.

All church going people everywhere take warning. Do not be fooled or lulled into sleep. Your church attendance and your church membership in and of itself does not qualify you into right relationship with Jesus Christ.

The only thing that counts is your personal relationship with Christ Jesus. Whosoever will call upon the name of Jesus shall be saved. Jesus is the only way to the Father. When we believe in our heart that Jesus died for our sins and rose again from the dead we shall be saved and then in right relationship with Jesus.

I hear the media often being offended implying that Christians are being "narrow minded" when they acknowledge that Jesus in not just one way – He is the

106 Peter Finds Purpose

only way to find restored relationship with God the
Father.

What their ignorance does not understand is that the
suffering of the Godhead was not just one of the choices
we were given to find our redemption. Does it make
sense to send Jesus to die on the cross if that suffering
and death in and of itself was not the sufficient and only
way of Salvation? If we had five ways to find our
salvation then God would just sit back and tell us to find
the other four and then would have spared His Son the
suffering, death and separation that Jesus experienced on
our behalf.

Sometimes we are so close or familiar with the church or
church language that we assume we must be all right in
the eyes of God. As I get older there is a larger sense in
my heart that I want to tread carefully and humbly before
by God. My heart is filled with gratitude as I accept the
love of God in my heart and all that He has done for me.
I choose not to presume or assume anything in Him. I
choose my salvation daily and recognize that only He
can keep me. I choose to not walk in my sinful nature
that dominated prior to Christ coming into my heart.

CHAPTER EIGHT
2 PETER 3

<u>2 Peter 3</u> *Beloved, I now write to you this second epistle (in BOTH OF which I stir up your pure minds by way of reminder), that you may be mindful of the words which were spoken before by the holy prophets, and of the commandment of us, the apostles of the Lord and Savior, knowing this first: that scoffers will come in the last days, walking according to their own lusts, and saying, "Where is the promise of His coming? For since the fathers fell asleep, all things continue as THEY WERE from the beginning of creation."*

For this they willfully forget: that by the word of God the heavens were of old, and the earth standing out of water and in the water, by which the world THAT then existed perished, being flooded with water. But the heavens and the earth WHICH are now preserved by the same word, are reserved for fire until the day of judgment and perdition of ungodly men.

But, beloved, do not forget this one thing, that with the Lord one day IS as a thousand years, and a thousand years as one day. The Lord is not slack concerning HIS promise, as some count slackness, but is longsuffering toward us, not willing that any should perish but that all should come to repentance.

The Day of the Lord

But the day of the Lord will come as a thief in the night, in which the heavens will pass away with a great noise, and the elements will melt with fervent heat; both the earth and the works that are in it will be burned up. Therefore, since all these things will be dissolved, what manner OF PERSONS ought you to be in holy conduct and godliness, looking for and hastening the coming of the day of God, because of which the heavens will be dissolved, being on fire, and the elements will melt with fervent heat? Nevertheless we, according to His promise, look for new heavens and a new earth in which righteousness dwells.

Be Steadfast

Therefore, beloved, looking forward to these things, be diligent to be found by Him in peace, without spot and blameless; and consider THAT the longsuffering of our Lord IS salvation—as also our beloved brother Paul, according to the wisdom given to him, has written to you, as also in all his epistles, speaking in them of these things, in which are some things hard to understand, which untaught and unstable PEOPLE twist to their own destruction, as THEY DO also the rest of the Scriptures.

You therefore, beloved, since you know THIS beforehand, beware lest you also fall from your own steadfastness, being led away with the error of the wicked; but grow in the grace and knowledge of our Lord and Savior Jesus Christ.

To Him BE the glory both now and forever. Amen.

Peter, in the very last words written and kept for us declares, "The reason I am writing this second book to you is to stir up your pure minds." He goes on to say, "Remember what the prophets of old said" as well as currently what Paul and his fellow apostles were preaching and warning at their end. **He warns** in the last days there will be **scoffers,** those that walk after their own lusts, **mocking** that the end had been promised but it has not been seen. But these are **willingly ignorant**, in other words they are choosing ignorance over the reality of God. And again Peter uses the terminology many will walk "after their own lusts." He brings this point up *eight times* in these two short epistles.

We cannot give the devil an inch in our hearts, our minds, or our actions. We so often think in daily life that this or that sin is "no big deal." But it is a big deal if lust in our hearts comes to conception and we sin. Even if the sin is a matter of the heart only! Just because sins are forgiven does not mean we have a license to sin.

Galatians 5:13 *For you, brethren, have been called to liberty; only do not use liberty as an opportunity for the flesh, but through love serve one another.*

Sometimes we misunderstand what sin does to us even when we know we are forgiven. It defiles our spirit and gets magnified in our own conscience. There are many Christians hampered in their own walk with the Lord because they cannot find personal victory or they struggle with some sin that so easily besets them. When your own conscience is plagued you lose some sense of purity and this becomes a stumbling block in your own heart. You then are unable to "tap into" the power of God because your conscience keeps reminding you of your shortcomings and failures.

Peter then goes on to tell us that contrary to whatever the scoffers tell us or the mockers mock us about it is the Word of God that has kept the heavens in place and kept the earth both in water and out of water. The same word keeps this earth today from the fire that is to come.

Time to God is nothing with a day the same as a thousand years and a thousand years as a day. Heaven and earth will pass away and we look for that day. It is a promise from God and it will happen. Peter says "don't fall from your steadfastness," but rather grow in the grace and the knowledge of Jesus Christ.

He then near the close brings things into startling perspective. He says this world around us is doomed as it is. That what has happened in life in terms of accomplishments or buildings or what seems important to us will all pass away. There will be nothing left of what we know now.

He then asks a rhetorical question. Since all of what we see will not last the question becomes; **"HOW SHALL WE THEN LIVE?"**

Peter says the only thing that matters is that we live in a holy manner and in the fear of the Lord while looking for the coming day of the Lord. He challenges us to be diligent and be without spot or blemish! Further he warns don't allow yourself to be led astray!

But he challenges us to grow in grace and in the knowledge of Jesus Christ. Grace is enablement by God to live for Him. The enablement of God is what we can lean on in the times of uncertainty. God's grace walks with us through tragedy. He is there when we are abused whether we see Him or not. He is there through the darkest of times and the best of times. If only we kept this life in heavenly perspective, we could see Him and hear Him, and know Him.

I knew a man once who had been sexually abused starting as a five year old through the time he was eight or nine. He always wondered why "God had let that happen? Why did God abandon him?" Sometime after he became a Christian and after much dealing with the pain forced upon him, one day in prayer he "looked back" at one of those moments of abuse. He saw Jesus in the room with tears in His eyes. He then realized that Jesus had not left him but was in fact there for him and cared for him. This realization brought great comfort and healing to his soul.

Next, the knowledge of Christ is an important admonition. The more we know Him the more His love will be understood. The more we can grasp His love for us the more motivated we will be to seek those things above while on earth in this current life. The more we know Him and who He is and how He works the greater peace we will have in this life. In the above experience by the abused little boy, we can realize that Jesus does not arbitrarily intervene in the normal course of life. He works through people as does the devil himself as in the case above. The sad thing was that that little boy had no human being looking out for him and protecting him.

Paul wrote to the Colossians summarizing for us what Peter's last words to us were all about: Not carnality but Christ's character expressed in our Christian life

Colossians 3:

*If then you were raised with Christ, **seek those things which are above**, where Christ is, sitting at the right hand of God. **Set your mind on things above**, not on things on the earth. For you died, and your life is hidden with Christ in God. When Christ WHO IS our life appears, then you also will appear with Him in glory.*

*Therefore **put to death your members which are on the earth: fornication, uncleanness, passion, evil desire, and covetousness, which is idolatry**. Because of these things the wrath of God is coming upon the sons of disobedience, in which you yourselves once walked when you lived in them.*

*But now you yourselves are to **put off all these: anger, wrath, malice, blasphemy, filthy language out of your mouth. Do not lie to one another**, since you have put off*

*the old man with his deeds, and have put on the new MAN who is renewed in knowledge according to the image of Him who created him, where there is neither Greek nor Jew, circumcised nor uncircumcised, barbarian, Scythian, slave NOR free, but **Christ IS all and in all.***

Character of the New Man

*Therefore, as THE elect of God, holy and beloved, put on tender mercies, kindness, humility, meekness, longsuffering; bearing with one another, and forgiving one another, if anyone has a complaint against another; even as Christ forgave you, so you also MUST DO. But above all these things put on love, which is the bond of perfection. And let the peace of God rule in your hearts, to which also you were called in one body; and be thankful. **Let the word of Christ dwell in you richly** in all wisdom, teaching and admonishing one another in psalms and hymns and spiritual songs, singing with grace in your hearts to the Lord. And whatever you do in word or deed, DO all in the name of the Lord Jesus, giving thanks to God the Father through Him.*

The Christian Home

Wives, submit to your own husbands, as is fitting in the Lord. Husbands, love your wives and do not be bitter toward them. Children, obey your parents in all things, for this is well pleasing to the Lord.

Fathers, do not provoke your children, lest they become discouraged.

Bondservants, obey in all things your masters according to the flesh, not with eyeservice, as men-pleasers, but in sincerity of heart, fearing God. And whatever you do, do it heartily, as to the Lord and not to men, knowing that from the Lord you will receive the reward of the inheritance; for you serve the Lord Christ. But he who does wrong will be repaid for what he has done, and there is no partiality.

If I were to sum up the two epistles of Peter in one sentence it would be this:

To all Christians everywhere – "It is not what you do for God but who you are that matters."

New King James Version used throughout. Big thanks to the great web site and resource: www.blueletterbible.org

Other books by Daryl T Sanders

Peter Finds Life – Analysis of Peter's journey as he walked with Christ as recorded in the Gospels

Peter Finds Power – Analysis of Peter's ministry as recorded in the Book of Acts

Why? Questions along the journey of life – Analysis of the Exodus and how the Children of Israel refused to see things as God saw them

God the Father – Analysis of why God chose to be known by Mankind as Father, discovering His functions in our relationship

David, Chosen by God – Analysis as to why David's name is in the Bible more than the name of Jesus, why does Jesus use David as a reference to who He is

Finding the Power to Heal – Analysis of how to tap into the faith that is in each of us to be healed.

Books are available at:

www.booksbydaryl.com

http://amzn.to/nIZJIJ

Or through Faith Fellowship in Ft. Myers, Fl
http://www.ffwom.org

Made in the USA
Charleston, SC
27 April 2012